More than just a great pilot and aircraft designer, Hughes was also instrumental in advancing commercial aviation. In the early 1930s, he began to purchase stock in Trans World Airways, a financially-troubled regional air carrier. Hughes eventually held a controlling interest in TWA, owning 74% of the company's stock.

Hughes, in his attempt to revive the ailing TWA, sketched preliminary design plans for a superior four-engine passenger plane. Lockheed agreed to build the "dream" plane if Hughes would foot the bill. The finished aircraft, the Lockheed Constellation, or "Connie," was far superior in size, speed, ceiling, and range than anything else in the air. Whenever Howard Hughes became personally involved in a project, it became something special, and this extended to his interest in helicopters. When the Aircraft Division of his company started producing a modest line of rotary-wing aircraft, Hughes took charge. His interest resulted in the XH-17, the world's largest helicopter. Perhaps no other single helicopter has done so much to revolutionize rotorcraft design.

Hughes' involvement in space exploration was equally significant. The first communications satellite to orbit the earth was a Hughes invention; the first U.S. soft landing on the moon was accomplished by a Hughes spacecraft, the Surveyor.

Howard Hughes' aviation achievements revolutionized the aircraft industry and helped create sophisticated, fast, and comfortable commercial transportation. Hughes had great dreams and brought them to reality.

After determining that the crash had been caused by a faulty hydraulic seal, Hughes redesigned the propeller configuration for the second prototype. The next test flight was successful, and the revised model was turned over to the military.

On November 2, 1947, Hughes piloted the last test flight of his career. Insisting he was doing only surface handling tests, Hughes revved up the eight massive engines of his enormous Hughes Flying Boat, the legendary *Spruce Goose*. With thousands of spectators on hand, Hughes lifted the giant aircraft into the air for a one-minute flight. The aircraft flew no higher than seventy feet and covered less than one mile, but it was the largest aircraft ever to have left the surface of the earth. This one-minute flight was a shining moment for Hughes. For years his critics had ridiculed him and his design, arguing that the "flying lumberyard" would never fly. Furthermore, they had accused Hughes of spending government money to build an airplane that he himself knew would never fly. After the flight, Hughes felt vindicated. And while the plane never performed the service for which it was originally intended, its successful test flight forever put an end to the critics and their scorn.

A SEQUOIA BOOK
OAK TREE PUBLICATIONS
SAN DIEGO, CALIFORNIA

HOWARD HUGHES
HIS ACHIEVEMENTS & LEGACY

The Authorized Pictorial Biography

N37602

Text by
ROBERT MAGUGLIN
WRATHER PORT PROPERTIES
LONG BEACH ● CALIFORNIA
Historical Consultant
BILL M. WINBERG

Produced for Wrather Port Properties by
Sequoia Communications, Inc.
Design by Jim Cook and Ron Rubenstein
Printed in Japan
ISBN: 0-86679-014-4 (pbk)
ISBN: 0-86679-024-1 (hdbk)
Library of Congress No. 85-050968

ACKNOWLEDGEMENTS

Many contributed to this publication and it is with appreciation and gratitiude
that we offer these acknowledgements:

Perry Lieber of the Summa Corporation; Richard Gano III of Wrather Port
Properties and his father Richard Gano II, for their guidance and counsel; John
McDonald of Hughes Aircraft; Knight-Harris and the staff of Producers Photo
Lab; Girard Louis Drouillard; Stan Soderberg; John Chance; Jewell Collage in
Liberty, Missouri; Ginny Brush; Mario Zamparelli; Bill M. Winberg, historical
consultant; Jim Cook of Cook/Sundstrom Associates for typesetting and design;
and Sequoia Communications.

And special thanks to those with vision who saw the magnitude of Howard Hughes'
life and achievements. For the preservation of this legacy in the Spruce Goose,
lasting appreciation goes most of all to Jack and Bonita Granville Wrather.

PHOTO CREDITS

KNIGHT HARRIS PRODUCERS PHOTO LAB: *copyright page.*
TIME MAGAZINE: *Opposite Table of Contents page.* BOONE INTERNATIONAL
CORPORATION: *8 (courtesy of John Chance).* G. BRUSH: *Cover.*
GIRARD LOUIS DROUILLARD: *49 top, 51, 52 bottom, 53 bottom, 54 top, 55
bottom, 116.* MARIO ARMAND ZAMPARELLI: *56.* PRIVATE COLLECTION: *106.*
HUGHES AIRCRAFT CO.: *109 top, 114.* HUGHES HELICOPTERS: *110, 111 top,
112.* SUMMA CORPORATION: *115.* ANDY WITHERSPOON: *116.*
HARA: *Inside back* ROBERT O. MAGUGLIN: *Back cover.*
WRATHER PORT PROPERTIES, LTD.: *All other photographs.*

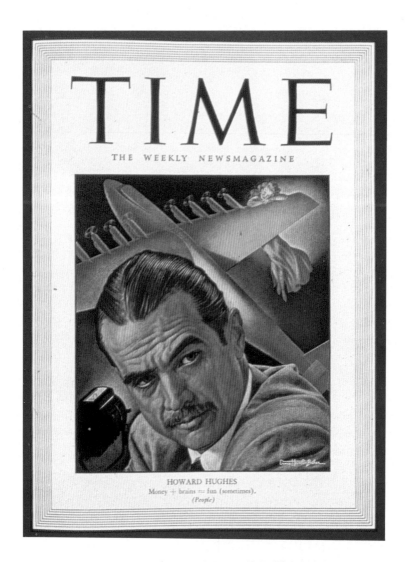

TIME

THE WEEKLY NEWSMAGAZINE

HOWARD HUGHES
Money + brains = fun (sometimes).
(People)

July 19, 1948, Time *magazine cover
story featured Howard Hughes'
flamboyant lifestyle. Article
highlighted Hughes' problems with
Senate investigators.*

Table of Contents

Hughes' ancestor, the Reverend John Gano, was chaplain of the Continental Army, and reputedly converted George Washington to the Baptist faith. This painting depicts the baptism in the Potomac River.

PART ONE:

The Early Years

The Hughes family line can be traced to the beginnings of colonial America. Jesse Hughes, of English-Welsh ancestry, arrived in America a few years after Jamestown was founded in 1607. He settled in Powhatan County, Virginia; as the colonial movement swept westward, the Hughes clan moved with it, settling in Kentucky, then Illinois, and finally, in 1853, in northeast Missouri.

Howard Hughes' great grandfather, Joshua W. Hughes, was granted forty acres of land in Scotland, Missouri, in return for government service as an Indian fighter. He build a log cabin and settled down to raise his family. His eldest son, Felix Hughes (Howard's grandfather), decided to teach school rather than take over the family farm.

After serving in the Union Army during the Civil War, however, he studied law and set up a practice in the tiny community of Lancaster, Missouri. He married a devout Southerner named Jean Amelia Summerlin; their marriage lasted sixty-one years.

Felix, a down-to-earth pragmatist, built a successful law career while Jean, dreamy and idealistic, lavished time, attention and money on their four children. Greta, the oldest, trained as an opera singer in Chicago, New York and Paris. Felix, Jr., the youngest, also had musical inclinations and went to Europe to study. Rupert, born in 1872, was so scholarly that he was nicknamed "History" by his family and friends. He received degrees from Adelbert College, in Cleveland, and from Yale. He wrote his first poem at age seven; it was the beginning of a successful literary career. He became an internationally famous author of popular fiction and later found success as a Hollywood screenwriter.

Only Howard, their second child (born in 1869) seemed unable to find his proper place in life. Although gifted with a mechanical mind, Howard soon earned an unsavory reputation for being rowdy and undisciplined. To please his father, Howard enrolled in law school but resented the tedium of legal study. Without finishing his law courses, he took—and passed—the Iowa Bar exam. He joined his father's law firm but soon found the quiet atmosphere of a law office unappealing. He decided to set out on his own.

He had an interest in mining and soon moved from one mining activity to another, seeking his fortune. He worked in zinc mining in the Indian territories, silver mining in Colorado, and lead mining in Missouri. Wherever he went, he could be found in the thick of things, having replaced his formal lawyer's clothing for the rough coveralls of the miners.

In January, 1901, Hughes heard of the great oil discovery at Spindletop, Texas. He soon left his lead mining operation in Missouri and found himself in the thick of the booming black gold industry. Later writing about his experiences, Hughes recalled, "I heard the roar in Joplin and made for the seat of

The infant Howard Hughes, born December 1905, in the arms of his mother, Allene Gano Hughes.

disturbance. Beaumont in those days was no place for a divinity student. The reek of oil was everywhere. It filled the air, it painted the houses, it choked the lungs and stained men's souls. Such another excitement will not be seen for a generation. It will take that length of time to get together an equal number of fools and 'come-ons' at one spot. I turned greaser and sank into the thick of it. Roughneck, owner, disowner, promoter, capitalist, and 'mark'—with each I can claim kin, for I have stood in the steps of each."

Hughes' fortunes came and went. One day he would have thousands in the bank, the next day he would be in debt. He was certainly not a good marriage prospect, but a young woman named Allene Gano was captivated by the dynamic young man and soon fell in love with him.

The Ganos traced their past to America's early history, as did the Hughes family; the Gano heritage, however, was more illustrious. The first Ganos in America were French Huguenots who fled religious persecution in France and arrived in New York during the seventeenth century.

The Reverend John Gano was chaplain of the Continental Army during the Revolutionary War. He is credited with converting George Washington to the Baptist Faith. General Richard Montgomery Gano was a successful doctor who gave up his medical practice to serve as a Confederate Cavalry officer during the Civil War. He fought in more than seventy battles, winning all but four. (During the war, five horses were shot from under him, but Gano was wounded only once.) He settled in Dallas after the war, where he preached the gospel, raised thoroughbred horses, and worked as a surveyor in Texas' uncharted lands.

General Gano's son, William Beriah Gano (the maternal grandfather of Howard Hughes, Jr.), graduated from Harvard Law School, practiced law and was elevated to judge soon after. He married Jeanette de Lafayette Grissim, or "Nettie," as she was affectionately called. A physician's daughter, she graduated from Wellesley College and also received a degree from the Musical Conservatory of Cincinnati. The Gano home, like the Hughes home, was a place of music and literature.

Hughes' mother's family, the Ganos, were an old, established family prominent in Texas affairs. Left to right standing: Robert E. Lee Gano, William Berial Gano (Howard Hughes' grandfather), Maurice Dudley Gano; seated: Emma Gano Scurry, Richard Montgomery Gano (Howard Hughes' great grandfather), Albert Sydney Johnson Gano, Kate Montgomery Gano McLaurin.

A playful young Howard Hughes lends a hand around the house.

Allene, born in 1883, was the oldest of William and Nettie's four children. Tall, with dark hair, she was quiet and sophisticated, seemingly a poor match for Howard Hughes, Sr. Nevertheless, Howard and Allene were married on May 24, 1904, after a brief courtship, at the Gano home in Dallas.

After an extended honeymoon in Europe, the newlyweds settled in the Houston area so Hughes could be near the center of the growing oil business. The once modest town was quickly developing as new buildings sprang up and steamers crowded the city's seaport.

Howard Robard Hughes, Jr., was born on Christmas Eve, 1905, in the family's small frame house at 1404 Crawford Street (just east of downtown Houston today). The birth was difficult for Allene; her doctor advised her against future childbirths.

The birth of Howard Hughes, Jr., was just as mysterious as his death seventy years later. Although

11

(Top left): W.B. Gano, Howard Hughes' grandfather, in 1903.
(Left): General Richard Montgomery Gano, Hughes' great-grandfather, served as a Confederate officer during the Civil War.

the attending physician, Dr. Oscar L. Norsworthy, was a respected doctor in the community and surely would have filed the necessary papers, there is no record of Hughes' birth at the Texas Division of Vital Statistics in Austin or at the Houston Board of Health. (Hughes discovered this problem himself when he needed proof of age during World War II; he was forced to submit affidavits from his aunt, Annette Gano Lummis, and from Estell Sharp, the mother of his closest friend.)

Little Howard, or "Sonny," as he was called by family and friends, had an unsettled first few years of life. With "Big Howard" jumping from one oil strike to another, Allene and Little Howard often found themselves packing and moving from town to town to be near the senior Hughes. Little Howard was just eighteen months old during one such move to Oil City, a boom town near Shreveport, Louisiana. While wildcatting in the nearby regions, big Howard was able to make extra money by doubling as postmaster and deputy sheriff of Oil City.

Hughes, Sr., then teamed with Walter Bedford Sharp, a talented and experienced oil man. (Sharp was an expert in oil field technology and created a patented process for injecting compressed air into wells in order to increase their flow.) Although the two partners worked well together, they made no profitable strikes of oil. The became increasingly frustrated with the current state of drilling equipment. The standard "fishtail" drill bits being used were sufficient for drilling in mud, sand and soft dirt, but were nearly useless aginst solid rock. Hughes and Sharp spent much of their time trying to solve this problem; many prospective strikes had to be abandoned when rock was encountered.

Finally, in 1908, Hughes discovered a marvelous invention, a rotary drill bit that could penetrate rock. The true story of its development may never be known because there are many versions. Walter Sharp's widow claimed her husband had a major role in the development of the bit, but the patent was listed only in Hughes' name. In the accepted version of the story, Hughes was found drinking in a Shreveport bar by a young millwright named Granville A. Humason. Humason showed Hughes a crude model of a drill bit made of wooden spools. The model was unique in that its two cone-shaped cutters would continue their cutting action while in contact with a tough surface such as rock. Humason had been unsuccessful in his attempts to sell the idea to other oil men, none of whom could understand the simple ingenuity of the device. Hughes, however, immediately realized the possibilities of the crude model. Humason offered the model to Hughes for the sum of $150, which Hughes paid on the spot. The exuberant Humason promptly spent $50 of his new-earned profits on a round of drinks for everyone in the bar. Hughes, however, had more important things on his mind.

Back in his workshop, he refined and elaborated the rough concept of this rotary bit and added much of his own creative genius to the device. He spent hours making scale drawings and specifications of the model and then sold a half-interest in the device to Sharp for $1,500. He used this money for a trip to Washington, D.C., where he hired an attorney to patent the Hughes Rotary Drill Bit.

In June 1909, Hughes and Sharp arrived at the oil

Howard Hughes, Sr., oversees work at a drilling site. His "rockeater" rotary drill was an instant success.

fields in Goose Creek, Texas, with a newly-fabricated prototype of the drill bit. At a hard-rock site that had previously stymied all conventional drill bits, Hughes and Sharp demonstrated the Hughes Drill Bit for the first time. Since the patent was not yet official, the two partners concealed the bit under a canvas cover and Hughes ordered all field hands away from the drilling platform. After attaching the bit to a standard rotary pipe stem, drilling began, and the drill bit's performance was nothing short of miraculous. In only eleven hours, the Hughes Rotary Drill Bit bore through fourteen feet of solid rock. The amazed oil men quickly dubbed their invention the "rock eater." A jubilant Hughes returned home, more eager than ever to secure the patent.

The increasingly successful Hughes moved his family back to Houston (Howard, Jr., was three at the time), residing on the city's prestigious south side. Although not yet in the category of the community's rich and powerful, Howard and Allene began to move in the city's elite social and cultural circles. They attended Christ Church Cathedral, the city's most distinguished Episcopalian church, and were members of the Houston Country Club.

The first school attended by young Howard was Prosso's Academy, a private school that catered to the city's wealthier families. Young Howard, like his father, displayed a general indifference toward formal education, earning only average marks. He was a painfully shy youth who spent most of his time alone, tinkering with mechanical gadgets. Even as a young child, Hughes showed a remarkable aptitude for mechanics and electronics. His father was delighted with his son's interests in mechanics and did his best to encourage the boy, hoping he would be inspired to attend college and earn an engineering degree. The older Hughes even set up a special work area for his son at the tool company's plant. Howard spent many happy hours there, working on his various projects.

He undertook one such project as a matter of necessity: his father refused to buy him a motorcycle. Howard took his own bicycle, assorted spare parts and a discarded motor and proceeded to build his own motorized bike. It was one of the first such contraptions in Houston, and a delighted Howard was the terror of the neighborhood as startled mothers herded their children to safety.

Young Howard also found electronics fascinating and soon built himself a working radio transmitter.

Four-year-old Howard shares a quiet moment with his mother.

Most of the working parts were obtained from the family's dismantled doorbell. Many years later, an adult Hughes recalled that one of his life's happiest moments was when he discovered that the crude transmitter actually worked.

As a young teen, Howard became increasingly involved in amateur radio and constructed a series of ham transceivers. With his shortwave radio equipment he contacted operators around the country and on ships at sea using his call sign, RCY. He even gathered together a group of fellow radio enthusiasts and formed the Radio Relay League, a local organization for amateur radio operators. Most of the meetings were conducted in Howard's room since he always owned the latest equipment.

During his childhood, the shy Hughes made only one real friend, Dudley C. Sharp, Walter Sharp's son. The boys were unlike in appearance and manner. Hughes was tall, thin, and pale while Dudley was strong and healthy. Where Howard was shy and withdrawn, Dudley was talkative and extroverted. Howard envied Dudley's ability to make friends and Dudley respected Howard's determination and mechanical prowess.

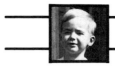

The two boys were best of friends. They even decided to learn how to play the saxophone together. After a short time, however, Dudley lost interest and gave it up; Hughes continued to play and practice into his adult life—a clear illustration of his drive and determination.

Introverted though he was, young Howard did not completely isolate himself from his peers. At the age of ten, he was crowned "King" of the Christ Church Cathedral May Fete. And, during that summer, he spent his first nights away from home, at Camp Teedyuskung in the Pocono Mountains in Pennsylvania. The camp was run by Daniel Carter Beard, one of the founders of the Boy Scouts of America. At the camp, boys were taught wilderness life and how to identify the flora and fauna. His mother hoped that the camp would strengthen her son's health, which had never been good. Of course, much of Howard's ill health may have been attributed to his mother's overprotectiveness. She was constantly worried about her son: she bombarded Beard with letters asking about his condition; she often sent long missives on how to care for him; she even sent newspaper clippings to Beard about polio epidemics on the East Coast. Allene was so worried that Howard might contract polio at camp that she picked him up on August 16 and took him to Cleveland to live with his Uncle Felix (his father's brother) until the polio scare was over.

The following summer, Howard looked forward to a return visit to camp, but Allene decided to keep him at home. When Howard fell ill with a digestive problem and lost nearly eight pounds, she abruptly changed her mind. She realized that the camp's hardy outdoor atmosphere might be just what the boy needed.

· On July 16, 1917, Howard and his good friend Dudley arrived at camp. But this year's experience was not much fun for Hughes; a group of camp bullies made life miserable for the younger boys. Despite this drawback, Allene was pleased with Howard's appearance at the end of the summer: he had put on weight and actually looked robust and healthy.

In 1919, Howard enrolled in Houston's South End Junior High School (later called San Jacinto High). His father was disappointed in Howard's consistently lackluster academic performance; he had high hopes for him to attend Harvard University. To this end, Howard, Sr., sent his son to a prestigious preparatory school the following year. In the fall of 1920, at age fourteen, Hughes arrived in Boston and enrolled in Fessenden School in West Newton, Massachusetts.

At Fessenden, young Howard surprisingly applied himself to his studies. That June, he was commended for "outstanding industry and attention to study," excelling in mathematics and working hard in languages, especially French. He also exhibited an entrepreneurial business flair: throughout the school year, Allene sent a steady supply of Texas grapefruit to Howard; he kept a small number for himself and sold the rest to his classmates for a nickel apiece.

Hughes' introverted nature still predominated, however. He did not make friends readily and seldom participated in the school's social functions. The slender Hughes did stand out among his peers in one respect, though: he was already the tallest boy in his class of thirty.

Hughes attended prestigious Fessenden Preparatory School in West Newton, Massachusetts, only one year before transferring to the Thatcher School in California's picturesque Ojai Valley.

Fifteen-year-old Howard at Fessenden School

During Howard's one year at Fessenden, he became passionately devoted to golf. He spent every available moment on the school's course. He entered the school championship and came in second, losing first place by one stroke.

Howard graduated from Fessenden's sixth form, the equivalent of eighth grade, in June 1921. By this time, Hughes, Sr., was spending more time on the West Coast looking after his oil business. As a result, he decided to send Howard to Thacher School in Ojai, California. Although Thacher's enrollment was full, Hughes managed to persuade the headmaster to admit his young son. Thacher was much smaller than Fessenden, with a total enrollment of sixty students. But even this intimate atmosphere did not help Howard overcome his shyness. He avoided group activities for the most part, although he did have a role in the school play as a detective. He bought a horse and spent many solitary hours riding in the hills surrounding the school.

On March 29, 1922, during Howard's spring semester at Thacher, his mother checked into Baptist Hospital in Houston for minor surgery. It was a routine operation, but for an unknown reason, complications arose. Allene never regained consciousness from the anesthetic. Her tragic and unexpected death—at the age of thirty-nine—devastated Hughes, Sr. After her death, he spent most of his time in New York and Los Angeles, stopping in Houston only when business made it necessary. When

he did go to Houston, he made it a point to avoid the family home on Yoakum Boulevard.

True to his nature, young Howard never openly expressed grief over his mother's death.

The older Hughes convinced Annette Gano, Allene's younger sister, to help raise his son. The three moved to Pasadena, California, where Hughes rented a cottage for Howard and Annette at the Vista del Arroyo Hotel, while he took rooms at the Ambassador Hotel, his favorite Los Angeles residence. Young Howard went back to Thacher School in the fall of 1922, but only for a short stay. Hughes, Sr., grief-stricken and lonely without his beloved wife, wanted his son near him. He arranged for Howard to attend the California Institute of Technology in Pasadena. (The school overlooked the fact that young Howard had not yet earned a high school diploma; chiefly because of his father's generous donation to the school.) Howard attended classes at Caltech but apparently received no official credit.

During this period, young Howard began to spend more time with his uncle, Rupert Hughes, who

15

already had a successful career as author of a series of popular novels; now, he worked as a screenwriter for Samuel Goldwyn. In fact, Rupert had become one of the most sought-after writers in the film community, earning more than $100,000 per year.

Rupert's parties were Hollywood institutions, attended by the town's most famous stars, writers, and producers. Young Howard was soon surrounded by the glitter and glamour of the Hollywood life-style. No one imagined that the shy young man standing in the corner was destined to become one of Hollywood's brightest stars.

During these months following his mother's death, young Howard experienced moviemaking on a first-hand basis. He spent many hours on movie sets with Rupert and observed the filmmaking process.

After one year in Los Angeles, Annette Gano announced that she wanted to move back to Houston. Hughes decided to enroll his son in Houston's Rice University so he could remain under Annette's care. Hughes, Sr., still chose to avoid Houston except for those rare times when business matters made a trip unavoidable.

One of those rare business meetings occurred on January 14, 1924. Hughes, Sr., attending a meeting with the tool company's manager, suddenly rose from his seat, clutched his heart, and collapsed. At age fifty-four, Howard Hughes, Sr., died from a massive heart attack.

For young Howard, his father's death came as a terrible shock. In less than two years, he had lost his mother and his father, both of whom apparently had been in good health. At age eighteen, Howard Hughes, Jr., found himself alone. His father had prepared a new will after Allene's death but had never signed it. The previous will left half of his estate to Allene, 25% to Howard, and the remainder to his parents and brother Rupert. Since Allene had passed away, her share now belonged to Howard; this gave him 75% of his father's tool company. Hughes wanted to supervise the business, but under Texas law, minors are considered unfit to run their own affairs. A court-appointed guardian would be assigned to Howard until he was twenty-one years old.

For Hughes, who had come to be very independent, this situation was intolerable, and he planned a different course of action. He discovered that under the Texas Civil Code, he could be declared a legal adult if he could prove to the court his competency in handling his own affairs. Hughes set out to prove just that.

He studied the business affairs of the Hughes Tool Company for hours so he could convince the judge that he had the ability to run a large company. And when it came time to appear in court, Hughes shrewdly scheduled it so that the judge hearing his case was one of his regular golfing partners.

Hughes filed the formal petition on his nineteenth birthday, December 24, 1924. Two days later, the judge signed the order and removed Hughes' "disabilities as a minor." At nineteen, Howard Hughes took over full control of the Hughes Tool Company. There had been one other problem—besides his age—that prevented Howard from obtaining full control. As mentioned, his father's will left 25% of the company to Rupert and the grandparents. But, in the months preceding his nineteenth birthday, which was the earliest time he could file his petition, Hughes instructed company management to buy out his relatives' minority shares. This act caused ill will and created a permanent breach between Hughes and his relatives, who had wanted him to go back to school.

Hughes left the competent managers of the tool company to run the business while he set out to plan his future. He already knew he wanted to move to California and produce motion pictures. He also wanted to pursue his growing interest in the science of aviation as well as experiment with steam-powered automobiles.

In the spring of 1925, Hughes began to court Ella Rice, the grand-niece of the founder of the prestigious Rice University. Ella was one of Houston's most sought-after debutantes and her family was at the top of the city's elite. Hughes' pursuit of the dark-haired, sophisticated Ella was rewarded; they were married on June 1, 1925. The ceremony, as proclaimed by the *Houston Chronicle,* was the "notable event of the year on the social calendar."

A dapper young Howard displays a rare smile for the camera.

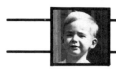

14-Year-Old Houstonian Invents Lighter and Cheaper Motorcycle

(Above) Five-year-old Howard displays latest in turn-of-the-century children's fashion.

(Left, top) Young Howard's inventiveness gained him notoriety at an early age.

(Left) Four-week-old Howard Hughes with grandfather W.B. Gano and great-grandfather Gen. Richard Gano.

Hughes family embarks on train excursion to Galveston, Texas.

(Left) Portrait photograph of Hughes at age ten; Keokuk, Iowa.

1911 at age six. Class picture at Miss Eichler's school in Houston. Hughes is in the second row. Ella Rice, Hughes' first wife, is seated in the second row, far left.

The sixteen-year-old Hughes became adept at handling horses during his attendance at Thatcher School in Ojai, California.

(Below) Hughes, a one-handicap golfer, played in many tournaments during the 1920s and 1930s. He is pictured here at age 18 while still living in Houston.

(Right) Hughes drove and owned many fine automobiles. This interest led to his later involvement in the development of a steam car.

(Far right) Hughes and his young bride, Ella Rice, shortly after their marriage in 1925, at a costume ball. The new Mrs. Hughes was a grand niece of William March Rice, the founder of Rice Institute.

Howard Hughes, Sr., a friend of the race- car driver
Barney Oldfield, behind the wheel of one of his
many autos.

Scores of spectators jammed Hollywood Boulevard during the 1930 premiere of Hughes' Hell's Angels *as a formation of World War I airplanes flew overhead and stuntmen parachuted onto the crowded street.*

PART TWO:

Hughes in Hollywood

Shortly after Hughes and Ella married, they moved to Los Angeles and took rooms at the Ambassador Hotel, his father's favorite West Coast residence. Hughes wanted to produce motion pictures. To this end, he spent many hours at the Goldwyn Studios in Culver City to learn all he could about the filmmaking process. Throughout his life, Hughes proved he could accomplish any goal he set for himself, and the moviemaking business was no exception.

Initiation into the film industry was a total disaster for Hughes, however. Ralph Graves, a popular actor and an old friend of his father's, approached Hughes with a story he thought would make a terrific movie. Howard placed his trust in Graves, rented a small studio, hired a crew and actors and let Graves do the rest. Hughes invested $60,000 in *Swell Hogan*, the story of a Bowery tough who adopts a baby. The naive Hughes believed he had produced a success, but he finally realized that the finished product was so bad that he made certain it was shelved. (Typical of Hughes' thoroughness, no known copy of the film exists.)

Another misjudgment of Hughes' that haunted him years later concerned a casting session for *Swell Hogan*. A very pretty but unknown young woman auditioned for a part in the movie. Hughes listened to her read and told her to look elsewhere for a movie role. She did just that. Clara Bow went on to become one of the screen's biggest stars.

The failure of *Swell Hogan* was just what everyone in Hollywood expected from the gangly youngster from Texas. But Hughes had acquired a taste for moviemaking and he fully intended to succeed in the business. He had a goal to accomplish.

Hollywood society was astonished when Hughes' very next film project succeeded. He was certain that the way to make money was to spend money, so he planned his next film venture carefully and invested $150,000 in it. Hughes hired an old friend of his father's, Marshall Neilan, to direct the new movie, called *Everybody's Acting,* and it received good reviews from the critics while returning a modest profit.

Hughes felt reassured by this minor success, so he and his bride moved out of the Ambassador Hotel and into a spacious Spanish-style house located at 211 Muirfield Road in Hancock Park. The back lawn of the house overlooked the fairways of the Wilshire Country Club, where Hughes often played golf.

To accommodate his expanding involvement in the film industry, Hughes modified the charter of one of his tool company subsidiaries, allowing it to produce motion pictures as well as lease drill bits. Thus, the Caddo Rock Drill Bit Company of Louisiana produced all of Hughes' early films.

Hughes set up West Coast offices for Caddo in the Taft Building, located at Hollywood and Vine. He hired a young accountant named Noah Dietrich to look after his business affairs. This proved to be one

Hughes with Dutch aircraft designer Anthony Fokker.

of Hughes' wisest decisions; Dietrich stayed with Hughes for nearly twenty years and helped shape the business into one of the world's largest personal fortunes.

The close-knit Hollywood elite considered the success of *Everybody's Acting* to be a lucky accident, though, and they did not yet take the young upstart seriously. But Hughes continued to amaze his most skeptical critics with one success after another.

He defied Hollywood's criterion for a box-office hit by producing a film without female leads. In fact, no women at all appeared in the movie, *Two Arabian Knights,* a comedy about the feud between a private and his sergeant set in the trenches of World War I. Hughes shrewdly signed director Lewis Milestone to a three-year contract, beginning with *Two Arabian Knights.* He invested the tremendous sum of $500,000 in the production, which was both a critical and a box-office success, and which won Milestone the Academy Award for Best Director in 1928 and made stars of its two leading actors, Louis Wolheim and William Boyd. Hollywood insiders began to reconsider their opinions of Howard Hughes.

After the success of *Two Arabian Knights,* Hughes searched for a film idea that would—once and for all—convince the world that he was an important filmmaker. Not surprisingly, Hughes decided to combine his love of moviemaking with his growing fascination with airplanes. He took a rough idea from Marshall Neilan and wrote a script about two World War I aviators.

From the very beginning, Hughes was determined that this film, *Hell's Angels,* would be no ordinary motion picture: it was to be an epic, his proof to a skeptical world that he was a master moviemaker. Perfection was his goal, no matter the cost, and he would see to it personally that everything met with his approval.

A team of scriptwriters took Hughes' outline and created a workable story line, set against the fiery backdrop of Europe's aerial warfare. Marshall Neilan was hired to direct; Ben Lyon and James Hall were cast as the two brothers who fall in love with the same girl; Greta Nissen, a beautiful Norwegian actress, was cast as the girl.

Almost immediately trouble developed between Hughes and Neilan. They argued over how the film should be shot. Neilan was fired and Hughes brought Luther Reed over from Paramount, but Reed didn't

Hughes poses for the camera outside box office at Two Arabian Knights *premiere in 1927.*

meet with any more success than had Neilan. Reed was enraged by Hughes' constant interferences. He quit, saying, "If you know so much, why don't you direct it yourself?" Hughes liked that advice and assumed the directing reins himself. He began to shoot the interior scenes on October 21, 1927, at Metropolitan Studio in Hollywood, completing them in two months.

However, the most important part of production was yet to be undertaken: the aerial battle sequences. Here, Hughes demanded total realism. He sent his agents across the country and to Europe in search of authentic World War I vintage aircraft. He spent

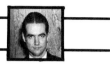
$500,000 on the purchase of eighty-seven bona fide fighter and scouting aircraft. He disdained the miniature models normally used for such aerial sequences. Hughes wanted to shoot his air battles with authentic aircraft under almost-real combat conditions. He searched for pilots and mechanics who could fly and maintain his air fleet. Eventually he hired 137 of the country's top aviators and stunt flyers, including the famous Roscoe Turner. With his perfectly restored airplanes and a full crew of pilots, Hughes found himself to be the commander of the world's largest private air force.

Unable to find an authentic German Gotha bomber for an important film sequence, Hughes bought Roscoe Turner's twin-engine Sikorsky, and his crew transformed it into a reasonable facsimile of the German plane. Since Hughes wanted everyone to believe the plane was an actual German bomber, the fake was kept a well-guarded secret.

Hughes gathered his air force together at Mines Field in Inglewood, California, in January, 1928. Sopwith Camels, SE-5's, Thomas Morse Scouts, Snipes, Avros, Canucks and Fokkers—all in mint condition—instantly recalled the real days of World War I. He then moved his fleet to a more spacious airfield in the San Fernando Valley to film the aerial sequences. Dozens of cameramen were used to shoot and reshoot scenes in order to capture the realism demanded by Hughes.

In his quest for authenticity, Hughes often asked his flyers to perform nearly impossible stunts. At times, nerves and tempers reached the boiling point. One pilot, who had performed a dozen low-level passes over a stationary camera, became enraged when Hughes signaled for yet another pass, this one even lower than the last. The angry pilot dove so low that his plane's undercarriage smashed the camera off its mount. Hughes was finally satisfied.

Famed aviator Roscoe Turner shakes hands with Howard Hughes after delivering giant "Gotha Bomber" for use in Hell's Angels.

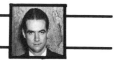

On another occasion, Hughes insisted that a Thomas Morse Scout biplane take off and immediately execute a sharp low-level turn. The stunt pilots insisted that this maneuver was impossible because the plane's rotary engine would cause it to spin and crash. Hughes disagreed and jumped into the tiny plane himself to prove the pilots wrong. At full throttle, he roared into the air and began his sharp left-hand turn. The stunt pilots were immediately proved correct: the Scout flipped into a spin and slammed into the ground. Hughes, unconscious, was pulled from the twisted wreckage. Fortunately he was not seriously injured, but he did sustain a crushed cheekbone that would plague him the rest of his life.

As a director, Hughes had clear visions of the footage he wanted and he would go to extreme lengths to get it. When he needed a backdrop of fluffy cumulus clouds and Southern California's clear skies refused to cooperate, Hughes flew his crew to the San Francisco area to get the shot.

The day before Hughes was scheduled to leave for San Francisco to make this shot, his wife left him and returned to Texas. Their marriage had never thrived because Hughes devoted all of his time to his various enterprises. As a young debutante, Ella Rice had been the belle of the ball, the center of an admiring cadre of social elite. Her husband's erratic hours and lack of attention were intolerable to her.

Hughes was undaunted by Ella's departure; instead, he finished shooting the final scenes for *Hell's Angels*. In the skies over the San Francisco Bay, he staged his epic air battle in which more than forty planes tumbled and wheeled in combat. These sequences became a masterpiece of aerial cinematography.

(Left, above) Director Howard Hughes with corps of stunt pilots during filming of Hell's Angels.

(Left, below) Thomas Morse Scout biplane crashed by Hughes while attempting low-level turn during the filming of Hell's Angels *in 1929.*

(Below) Hughes directs Ben Lyon and Jean Harlow in Hell's Angels *sequence.*

The crew moved back to Los Angeles where one major scene remained to be shot. In it, the giant Gotha bomber, damaged by Allied artillery fire, bursts into flames and spins downward to earth where it crashes and burns, a fitting symbol of the fall of the mighty German war machine.

As usual, Hughes insisted on total authenticity. He decided to actually destroy Roscoe Turner's Sikorsky in a real crash. The pilots tried to convince Hughes not to spin the big plane because it was such a dangerous maneuver, but Hughes was adamant, and finally a brash young pilot named Al Wilson agreed to pilot the plane for the climactic scene. Another man was needed to light smoke pots in the fuselage so the plane would appear to be on fire. Phil Jones, a mechanic eager to learn to fly, volunteered to light the fuses. Both men donned parachutes and would bail out when the plane began its final spin.

Hughes filmed the action from a small plane flying alongside the Sikorsky. Wilson jerked the lumbering plane into an awkward spin at 5,000 feet and bailed out. Jones lit the fuses but remained in the plane. Either he missed the signal to jump or he was unable to bail out. The Sikorsky slammed to the ground with Jones still on board. Hughes landed quickly in a nearby field and rushed to the burning plane to pull Jones out, but it was too late: Jones was dead. Few moviegoers ever realized that the final scene of *Hell's*

Adolphe Menjou, Mary Brian, and Pat O'Brien in a scene from Hughes' hit movie, Front Page.

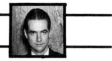

Angels was an actual accident in which a man was killed. Three men ferrying aircraft cross-country had died while *Hell's Angels* was in pre-production, but Jones's death was the only fatality during actual filming.

Hughes was prepared to release his masterpiece in 1929, but his silent film had become obsolete: Al Jolson had made his talking appearance in *The Jazz Singer* and talkies were now the rage. Hughes, not to be outdone, decided to reshoot *Hell's Angels*—with sound. The aerial sequences were easy: actual engine noises could be dubbed onto a sound track. For this task, Hughes hired Pancho Barnes, the famous woman pilot. In her high-powered plane she buzzed a barrage balloon rigged with microphones so that authentic engine noises could be recorded.

Actors Ben Lyon and James Hall would still work as the male leads because their voices were suitable, but the female lead, Greta Nissen, spoke with a heavy Norwegian accent and was unsuitable for the role of the English girl with whom the pilots fall in love.

After a quick and massive search, Hughes chose a sensual blonde named Harlean Carpenter, a bit-part actress who had never had a major film role. *Hell's Angels* was the first starring role for the girl, who became one of Hollywood's greatest sex symbols.

Hughes, displaying keen publicity skills, changed the actress's name to Jean Harlow and even coined the phrase "platinum blonde" to describe her hair. Casting Harlow was perfect for the picture. When she uttered her memorable line, "Do you mind if I slip into something more comfortable?", her career as a Hollywood sex goddess was launched. Later, thousands of women across the country rushed to beauty parlors to dye their hair platinum blonde.

Hell's Angels was finally completed in 1930. Hughes had shot 2.5 million feet of film (the final version contained only 15,000 feet), employed more than 20,000 people, and spent more than $3.8 million. It was the most expensive movie ever made until David O. Selznick decided to burn Atlanta for *Gone With The Wind*.

For the Hollywood premiere of the movie, Hughes' publicity talents emerged again. The film's lavish opening—on June 20, 1930—awed even the most jaded Hollywood cynic. A squadron of World War I planes flew over Grauman's Chinese Theater while stunt men jumped from the planes' wings and parachuted onto Hollywood Boulevard. (Actually, the first private screening of the film, supposedly for

Hughes alone, generated as much publicity as the gala premiere: Louella Parsons, the queen of Hollywood gossip, snuck into the theater and saw the film in its entirety.)

Hell's Angels was a smashing success. The critics loved it and people lined up to buy tickets for "the greatest movie ever made."

While working on *Hell's Angels,* Hughes also produced two lesser-known films, *The Mating Call* and *The Racket.* Neither was a box office hit. After the overwhelming success of *Hell's Angels,* Hughes went back to producing; he hired others to direct and edit his productions.

In the year after *Hell's Angels,* Hughes produced five pictures: *The Age for Love, Cock of the Air, Sky Devils, The Front Page,* and *Scarface. Cock of the Air* featured Hughes' latest love interest, Billie Dove. He tried to capitalize on the popularity of *Hell's Angels,* but the film was not well received. *Sky Devils,* another flying picture, died at the box office, as did *The Age for Love,* a comedy chosen to highlight Billie Dove's talents.

Hughes did have two big successes after Hell's Angels, however. *The Front Page,* which introduced Pat O'Brien, was the story of a prisoner who escapes by borrowing the sheriff's pistol during the reenactment of a crime. This screen version of the Ben Hecht-Charles MacArthur play was directed by Lewis Milestone. Hughes gave Milestone full control except for some casting decisions, several of which would haunt Hughes for years. (He turned down two unknowns for the lead role: James Cagney, whom Hughes called "a little runt," and Clark Gable, whose "ears make him look like a taxicab with both doors open.") The film was critically acclaimed and is considered to be Hughes' best effort as a filmmaker.

His other success was *Scarface,* a spin-off of Al Capone. Paul Muni starred in the title role with George Raft and Boris Karloff as supporting actors. Howard Hawks directed. The completed picture was bloody and violent and even hinted at an incestuous relationship between Scarface and his sister. The Motion Picture Producers and Distributors of America, Hollywood's censoring agent, promptly rejected the film, barring its release. The board demanded substantial cuts in the film, including a complete rewrite of the ending. (Instead of Scarface being gunned down by police, the board wanted him to be captured and brought to trial.) Hughes at first attempted to compromise with the board but then

became enraged at its interference and flatly refused to make any changes. He issued a statement condemning the censorship of free expression by "self-styled guardians of the public welfare" and accused the censors of being politically motivated. Hughes won many admirers for his courageous defense of free expression, and after a series of lawsuits, he won his case. *Scarface* was distributed with its original ending. It was a box-office smash and won critical praise as well.

After *Scarface,* Hughes turned his attention to his first love: aviation. Ten years passed before Hughes again personally took part in one of his film productions.

Not surprisingly, when Hughes finally returned to moviemaking, the subject stirred worldwide attention and controversy. The movie, titled *The Outlaw,* was a Western based loosely on the life of Billy the Kid. In the film, the ruthless outlaw is portrayed as a romatic

Another Hughes discovery, Paul Muni, starred in the controversial gangster film, Scarface.

One of Hughes' discoveries, the seductive Jane Russell, as she appeared in The Outlaw.

hero. Billy was played by Jack Beutel, a twenty-one-year-old unknown actor, and the female lead was played by a well-endowed dentist's receptionist and aspiring actress named Jane Russell.

Director Howard Hawks quit due to Hughes' interference, so Hughes directed the film himself. He seemed to go to great lengths to insure that the film shock the public and enrage the censors. One scene found Beutel and Russell in bed together, for purely "medicinal purposes." Hughes also designed a special bra to accentuate Russell's natural curves. Jokes abounded about Hughes and his aerodynamically cantilevered bra!

When Hughes tried to release the picture, the censors banned it. They demanded that large sections of the film be cut. Hughes refused and shelved the picture for nearly three years while he underwent legal and media battles with the censors. The publicity generated by Hughes turned Jane Russell into a household name years before anyone saw her on the silver screen.

In May 1948, Hughes purchased a controlling interest in RKO Pictures. The deal included 24% of the RKO stock and gave Hughes control of sound stages at studios in Hollywood and Culver City, a ranch in Encino and 124 movie theaters.

Howard Hughes the Playboy

In 1925, when Howard Hughes decided to make motion pictures, the film community treated him with disdain. But after the huge success of *Hell's Angels,* he suddenly found himself courted by Hollywood's most powerful and famous personalities. He was swept into the glamour of filmdom's inner circles. Awkward and ill at ease in crowds, the shy and gangly Hughes was an unlikely candidate for his movie-mogul role. Nevertheless, he was invited to some of the community's most exclusive get-togethers.

Hughes spent many weekends at Casa Encantada, the fabulous San Simeon castle owned by publisher William Randolph Hearst. Hearst and his constant companion, Marion Davies, were noted for hosting lavish parties, the guest lists of which read like a Who's Who of Hollywood. (One such party included Douglas Fairbanks, Charles Chaplin, Mary Pickford, Norma Shearer, Irving Thalberg, and Louis B. Mayer.) A private train transported the party-goers from Los Angeles to San Luis Obispo, where a fleet of limousines took them to Hearst's mountain hideaway that overlooked the Pacific Ocean.

Following his divorce, Hughes was Hollywood's most eligible bachelor, appearing in public with many actresses. Here he is seen at dinner with Ginger Rodgers.

Hearst enjoyed costume parties and went to elaborate lengths to decorate his home in the appropriate theme. An existing photograph shows a smiling Hughes decked out in lederhosen at a Bavarian-style party. He is seated with Eileen Percy, Kay English, Ricard Boleslawsky, Jack Warner and Marion Davies. Hughes and Ms. Davies, who lived with Hearst, got along well together; they shared a passion for ice cream and often had contests to see who could eat the most. Davies was responsible for introducing Hughes to Billie Dove, starting a passionate relationship that lasted many years. In fact, many believe that Dove was the one real love of Hughes' life.

Throughout the 1930s and 1940s, Hughes was romantically linked with dozens of women. One who enjoyed a very special relationship with him was Katharine Hepburn. They shared many interests, including golfing and flying. Hughes pursued

(Below) Hughes with Hollywood friends in Tyrolian garb at a party thrown by William Randolph Hearst on October 26, 1934. Seated to Hughes' left are actress Marion Davies and producer Jack Warner.

(Right) Dressed for golf, Hughes poses with Jack Gaines in February 1928 at the Los Angeles Municipal Golf Course in Griffith Park.

Hepburn diligently and even built a landing strip near her summer home in Connecticut.

Terry Moore, also an actress, claimed—after Hughes death—that he had married her in a secret ceremony aboard his yacht, although no evidence exists to substantiate her claim. Other actresses romantically linked with Hughes include Faith Domergue, Carole Lombard, June Lang, Linda Darnell, Anne Francis, Bette Davis, Lana Turner, Virginia Mayo, Ida Lupino, Joan Fontaine, Shelley Winters, Ava Gardner, Yvonne DeCarlo, Olivia De Havilland, Gina Lollobrigida, Janet Leigh, Mitzi Gaynor, Loretta Young, Elizabeth Taylor, Susan Hayward, and Audrey Hepburn. Most of the rumors linking Hughes with these Hollywood beauties are unfounded, though; they were publicity stunts created to promote the actresses' careers, because wherever Hughes went, the cameras and newsmen went too.

(Above) A tuxedoed Hughes shares a table with Beatrice Hudson and Katherine Barker at the Annual Victory Ball held at the Waldorf-Astoria in New York City. Hughes was romantically linked with some of Hollywood's biggest names, including Katherine Hepburn (top left) and Billie Dove (top right). The former was one of Howard Hughes' favorite photographs and was found among his personal effects.

35

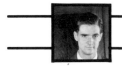

(Above) Hughes chats with actress Veronica Lake and actors William Powell and Andre Toth at the 21 Club in New York City on February 17, 1946. Johnny Meyer, head of Howard Hughes' public relations, is seen in the background.

(Left) Hughes talks with opera singer Lily Pons and columnist Lucius Beebe at the Beverly Wilshire Hotel in Los Angeles on November 8, 1938.

(Right) Actress Bette Davis smiles at Howard Hughes. They are pictured here at the Tailwagger's Dinner Dance in Holly-wood on August 13, 1938.

(Left) Howard Hughes is pictured with Mary Lansing (left), Minerva Ray Dean, and Robert Gill.

(Below) Pat Dicco, June Knight, and Howard Hughes dine together at the Beverly Wilshire in 1935.

(Right) Hughes with Ava Gardner at Joe Louis and Tomi Mauriello fight at Madison Square Garden, New York, 1946.

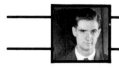

(Above) Stunt Pilots flew World War I biplanes in realistic aerial combat sequences for Hell's Angels. *Here, one pilot flies over the San Fernando Valley, June 1929.*

(Right, above) Harry Parry, stunt pilot and coordinator, diagrams aerial maneuvers for director Hughes on location for Hell's Angels.

Hell's Angels *stunt pilots line up before the largest fleet of World War I airplanes ever assembled for the making of a motion picture. This event took place on the runway of the Oakland Airport, March 15, 1929.*

Hell's Angels, *the most expensive film of its period, cost $4 million and employed as many as 20,000 cast and crew members.*

(Above) Director Hughes relaxes in the director's chair on location in Van Nuys, March 20, 1928. Star Jean Harlow (inset) poses with luggage next to airplane.

(Below) Stunt pilots are pictured in front of huge Sikorsky, which played the part of a German Gotha bomber in the film.

The Outlaw, *starring the statuesque Jane Russell, stirred the anger of the censors and the public interest with its daring closeups of Ms. Russell. Hughes (right) directed the film and personally coordinated the publicity campaign, which brought millions to the box office.*

Howard Hughes Filmography

1925—

SWELL HOGAN
Directed by Ralph Graves
Produced by Howard Hughes
Note: Picture was not released.

1926—

EVERYBODY'S ACTING
Paramount
Directed by Marshall Neilan
Produced by Howard Hughes
*Cast: Betty Bronsen, Ford Sterling, Louise Dresser, Henry
    Walthal, Raymond Hitchcock*

1927—

TWO ARABIAN KNIGHTS
United Artists
Directed by Lewis Milestone
Produced by Howard Hughes
*Cast: William Boyd, Louis Wolheim, Mary Astor, Boris
    Karloff*
*Note: Lewis Milestone won an Academy Award for this
    film.*

1928—

THE MATING CALL
Paramount
Directed by James Cruze
Produced by Howard Hughes
Cast: Thomas Meighan

THE RACKET
Paramount
Directed by Lewis Milestone
Produced by Howard Hughes
Cast: Thomas Meighan, Marie Proust, Louis Wolheim

1930—

HELL'S ANGELS
United Artists
Produced and directed by Howard Hughes
Cast: Jean Harlow, Ben Lyon, James Hall
*Note: Production started in 1927 and was originally filmed
    as a silent picture. Much of the footage was re-shot
    with sound.*

1931—

COCK OF THE AIR
United Artists
Directed by Lewis Milestone
Produced by Howard Hughes
Cast: Billie Dove, Chester Morris, Matt Moore

THE FRONT PAGE
United Artists
Directed by Lewis Milestone
Produced by Howard Hughes
*Cast: Adolphe Menjou, Pat O'Brien, Mary Brian, Edward
    Everett Horton, Walter Catlett*

THE AGE FOR LOVE
United Artists
Directed by Frank Lloyd
Produced by Howard Hughes
*Cast: Billie Dove, Edward Everett Horton, Charles Stewart,
    Lois Wilson, Mary Duncan*

1932—

SKY DEVILS
United Artists
Directed by Edward Sutherland
Produced by Howard Hughes
Cast: Spencer Tracy, William Boyd, George Cooper

SCARFACE
United Artists
Directed by Howard Hawks
Produced by Howard Hughes
*Cast: Paul Muni, George Raft, Ann Dvorak, Karen
    Morley, Boris Karloff*

1943—

THE OUTLAW

United Artists
Produced and directed by Howard Hughes
Cast: Jane Russell, Jack Beutel, Thomas Mitchell, Walter
*   Huston*
Note: Production was started in 1940. Release was delayed
*   almost two years due to censorship problems.*

1947—

MAD WEDNESDAY

United Artists
Produced and directed by Preston Sturges
Cast: Harold Lloyd, Frances Ramsden, Jimmy Conlin,
*   Lionel Stander, Rudy Vallee*
Note: Original title, "The Sin of Harold Diddlebock"

(The following films were produced by RKO Studios during Howard Hughes' reign at the studio and represent only those productions in which he was involved in some form or another. An asterisk indicates a *special* involvement of Hughes in the film.

1949—

THE CLAY PIGEON
THE BIG STEAL
FOLLOW ME QUIETLY
STRANGE BARGAIN
A DANGEROUS PROFESSION
THE THREAT
HOLIDAY AFFAIR

1950—
THE OUTLAW* *(Re-issue)*
ARMORED CAR ROBBERY
THE WHITE TOWER
WHERE DANGER LIVES*
BUNKO SQUAD
BORN TO BE BAD
MAD WEDNESDAY* *(Re-issue)*
NEVER A DULL MOMENT
VENDETTA*

1951—
HUNT THE MAN DOWN
THE COMPANY SHE KEEPS
GAMBLING HOUSE
MY FORBIDDEN PAST
BEST OF THE BAD MEN
ROADBLOCK
FLYING LEATHERNECKS
HIS KIND OF WOMAN
THE WHIP HAND
THE RACKET* *(Remake of his 1928 film)*
TWO TICKETS TO BROADWAY*
DOUBLE DYNAMITE*

1951—
ON DANGEROUS GROUND
A GIRL IN EVERY PORT
LAS VEGAS STORY*
AT SWORDS POINT
THE PACE THAT THRILLS
MACAO*
THE HALF BREED
THE NARROW MARGIN
ONE MINUTE TO ZERO
MONTANA BELLE *(Produced by Republic Studios,*
*   Hughes loaned Jane Russell to Republic, then later*
*   bought the picture and released it through RKO.)*
BLACKBEARD THE PIRATE

1953—
ANGEL FACE
SPLIT SECOND
AFFAIR WITH A STRANGER
SECOND CHANCE* *(3-D)*
DEVIL'S CANYON *(3-D)*

1954—
THE FRENCH LINE* *(3-D)*
SHE COULDN'T SAY NO
DANGEROUS MISSION
SUSAN SLEPT HERE

1955—
UNDERWATER* *(Superscope)*
SON OF SINBAD

1956—
*THE CONQUEROR

1957—
*JET PILOT

*Note: Hughes sold his interest in RKO in July 1955. Both *The Conqueror* and *Jet Pilot* were started prior to that date.

Mementos of the Hughes Legacy

When Howard Hughes died in 1976 he left the world an unparalleled legacy of achievement. In 1981, the design team working on the creation of the Spruce Goose exhibition discovered that Mr. Hughes had bequeathed more than just memories. Locked behind steel-doored vaults in a guarded warehouse in Los Angeles, Howard Hughes' most coveted personal mementos lay stored. Each item had been carefully wrapped and placed in boxes or heavy packing crates. As each vault was opened, researchers were rewarded with new treasures. Hughes' pilot logbooks, trophies, medals, citations, and even his golf clubs had been packed away, as though patiently awaiting Hughes' return.

Howard Hughes lived his life during a marvelous era of aeronautical and technological advancement: his mementos represent a vital link to a proud heritage of accomplishment. Dozens of these items from Mr. Hughes' personal collection are now on display in special glass cases in the Spruce Goose Dome in Long Beach. Each item is a thought-provoking time capsule capable of turning back the clock to the great days when there were frontiers to challenge and great men to challenge them.

Howard Hughes' dynamic personality, strength and ability allowed him to effectively advance the technology of his day to meet with tomorrow's needs. This collection of precious reminders serves to reintroduce today's audience to the true nature of Mr. Hughes' achievements in aviation, commercial transportation, electronics, space technology, movie-making, and finance.

The original 1908 patent for the Hughes "rockeater" drill bit.

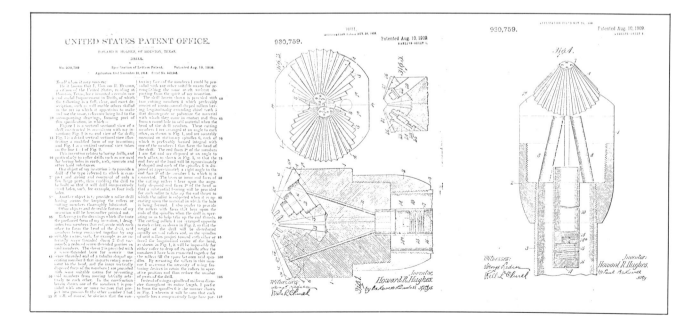

(Right) The revolutionary Hughes drill bit used three rotary cutters to chew through rock.

(Below) Hughes visits the Hughes Tool Company plant in Houston, Texas, and examines a new rock bit head; July 30, 1938.

Hughes' first great publicity campaign leading up to the premiere in 1930 sold the film Hell's Angels. *Publicity posters at left and above highlight the film's combination of action and romance.* Hell's Angels *propelled actress Jean Harlow (left) to super-stardom.*

Golf was one of Hughes' great passions. He had a photographer film his swing and then reviewed the motion picture footage to improve his style. Hughes won numerous trophies as an amateur golfer.

Hughes received many awards for aeronautical achievement: (below) an award from the Ligue International de Aviateurs, World Champion Aviator, 1938.

(Right) Hughes stands alongside his H-1 racer, which he designed and built in 1935.

(Below) The Collier Trophy, awarded to Hughes for his record-breaking flights, including those made in his H-1 racer and the Northrup Gamma.

(Below, right) An oil painting of H-1 in flight illustrates the craft's stream-lined appearance. This painting is now on display with the Collier Trophy and other Hughes Aviation mementoes at the Hughes Flying Boat exhibit in Long Beach, California.

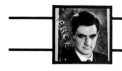

(Above) Hughes engineers developed this special telephone amplifier to aid the increasingly hard-of-hearing Hughes. Hughes used the telephone console at his Beverly Hills home during the war years.

(Left) Special cold weather flying gear for around-the-world flight.

(Below) Hughes emerges from the cockpit of his H-1 racer after setting the new trans-continental speed record.

left)   A triumphant Hughes strides ashore after successful test of Hughes Flying Boat on November 2, 1947.

(Below, left) A Congressional medal, awarded to Hughes, was minted in honor of the Round-the-World flight in 1938.

(Below, right) Jacket and famous brown fedora worn by Howard Hughes during the flight of the Spruce Goose.

Portrait of Howard Hughes by the designer, Mario Armand Zamparelli.

PART THREE:

Aviation to 1940

Few Americans realize the extent to which aeronautical science was furthered due to Howard Hughes' obsessive genius. His achievements in aviation are staggering: in addition to being a gifted pilot who broke dozens of world flight records, he was also a brilliant aircraft designer who was instrumental in advancing commercial aviation in the United States.

He won every major aviation award, including a special Congressional Medal, the Harmon Trophy, and the Collier Trophy. He was a charter member of the Aviation Hall of Fame. He owned a controlling interest (74%) of TWA, one of the world's largest and most prosperous airlines. The Hughes Aircraft Company has become one of the nation's most important suppliers of high technology electronic equipment, missiles and guidance systems. Hughes Helicopters is a major supplier of commercial and military rotary-wing aircraft. Hughes also provided an impetus for a worldwide weather reporting system and participated in many early experiments in aircraft navigation and safety equipment.

Hughes' life-long love affair with planes began at an early age. As a child, he was fascinated by all things mechanical. Considering this preoccupation, it came as no surprise that a teenaged Hughes was captivated by this century's most wondrous mechanical device, the flying machine.

Young Howard's first taste of flying came at age fourteen, while he was a student at Fessenden School in Massachusetts. He watched the Harvard-Yale boat race with his father, a Harvard man, who told him that if Harvard won the race, whatever his son wanted was his. When Harvard won, the elder Hughes was shocked to learn that his son wanted a ride in an airplane. As an adult, Hughes recalled the incident: "I asked to be permitted to fly with a pilot who had a broken-down seaplane anchored on the river in front of the hotel. My father finally consented. That was my very first contact with flying. I remember the airplane very well. It was a *Curtiss* flying boat. Not a land plane on pontoons but a single-hull flying boat, and the engine was overhead. It was a biplane and I am quite sure it was a pusher—the engine ahead of the propeller. If remember right, it was an Ox-5 V-8." Clearly, the event left a lasting impression on the young man.

Hughes had little formal education in engineering. He taught himself aviation science and was so thorough that many noted engineers later attested to Hughes' remarkable grasp of aerodynamic principles.

Hughes' first active involvement in aviation coincided with the start of his most famous film, *Hell's Angels*. Production on the film started in 1927, and in that year, Hughes began systematic flight training at Clovis Field in Santa Monica, California. His instructor was Charles Lajotte, an Army-trained aviator who, at twenty-two, was the same age as Hughes. According to Lajotte, Hughes was "a terrific pilot...he wasn't interested in just soloing; he was there to learn all he could from me."

Radio newsman interviews Hughes at the end of his record-breaking transcontinental flight in the H-1 racer. The 1937 flight broke his own 1936 Northrup Gamma record.

UNITED STATES OF AMERICA
DEPARTMENT OF COMMERCE
OFFICE OF THE DIRECTOR OF AERONAUTICS

PILOT'S IDENTIFICATION CARD

This Identification Card, issued on the
16th day of Nov. , 19 28 accompanies
Pilot's License No. 4223

Age 23
Weight 150 Color hair Brown
Height 6'3" Color eyes Brown

FORM R-19   Pilot's Signature.

UNITED STATES OF AMERICA
DEPARTMENT OF COMMERCE
OFFICE OF THE DIRECTOR OF AERONAUTICS
FORM R-18

OFFICIAL NO. 4223

This Certifies, That Howard R. Hughes

whose photograph and signature accompany this license,
is a **TRANSPORT PILOT**
of civil aircraft of the United States and entitled to the
privileges of all classes of licensed pilots.
Unless sooner suspended or revoked this license expires

May 15, 1929

Director of Aeronautics.

*(Above) Howard Hughes' pilot license,
showing his rating for transport
aircraft.*

*(Right) Hughes unloads baggage while
working as a copilot for American
Airways under the name of Charles
Howard.*

By the end of 1927, Hughes had earned his private pilot's license. By August, 1928, he held a commercial rating. Soon after, he added multi-engine and instrumental ratings. He bought a *Waco* biplane, which he flew for hours over Southern California to log flying time and gain valuable experience.

Hughes' first air crash occurred during the filming of *Hell's Angels* when a stunt pilot told him that a steep left-hand turn could not be performed. The stunt pilot, Frank Clarke, told Hughes that the gyro forces of the *LeRhone* rotary engine would force him into the ground in such a turn. Unconvinced, Hughes climbed into the cockpit of the plane and roared skyward to prove that the stunt was possible. It wasn't. The plane, as predicted, spun to the ground. Hughes was pulled—unconscious—from the wreckage. Fortunately he was not seriously hurt.

All in all, Hughes took great delight in making *Hell's Angels*. It allowed him to collect the largest private air force in the world—eighty-seven vintage World War I aircraft.

In the summer of 1932, with *Hell's Angels* on its way to a successful box-office run, Hughes suddenly vanished. Even close associates denied knowledge of his whereabouts. Two months later, the mystery ended when a young American Airways copilot turned out to be none other than the millionaire Howard Hughes. Hughes had applied for and was accepted as a copilot by American Airways under the pseudonym Charles Howard. He flew *Fokker* tri-motor transports on the Fort Worth-to-Cleveland run, and later, in 1935, flew DC-2's on TWA's transcontinental runs.

Hughes had first earned his pilot's license in a *Waco* cabin biplane. But the awkward craft was slow

and cumbersome and Hughes soon developed a passion for speed and performance. It seemed that no ordinary plane could live up to his expectations.

Finally, in 1932, through a special agreement with the Army Air Corps and the Boeing Aircraft Company, Hughes purchased a Boeing model 100A, a two-seat, open cockpit biplane. It was the civil version of the Army's P-12B and the Navy's F4B. Boeing had developed the airplane, and its performance was so sensational that both the Navy and the Army owned versions of the aircraft.

Hughes bought his Model 100A for $45,000. Sensational airplane or not, Hughes intended to improve its performance. He devised a detailed plan for modifying the swift pursuit ship and contracted Douglas Aircraft Company to do the work. Hughes redesigned the airplane's wing and tail geometry and reduced it from a two-seater to a single seat. He replaced the engine with a more powerful 450 horsepower Pratt and Whitney engine and streamlined the nose cowling to decrease drag. When the modifications were finally completed, the $75,000 price tag for the redesign exceeded the plane's original purchase price.

Hughes competed in the Miami Air Races in 1934 with his modified Boeing Model 100, in which he won his first aviation trophy, the Trujillo Trophy.

At this time, Hughes purchased another aircraft, a twin-engine Sikorsky S-38 amphibian. As usual, Hughes was not completely satisfied and required extensive modifications. The man placed in charge of the conversion at Pacific Airmotive was a young mechanic named Glenn Odekirk. When the changes were completed, Hughes hired Odekirk to be copilot and mechanic on an extended flying tour in the Sikorsky.

Hughes and Odekirk embarked on an aerial adventure reminiscent of Tom Sawyer's famous raft trip down the Mississippi. They left Los Angeles in February 1933, and flew the S-38 to Phoenix, then to Houston for a tour of the Hughes Tool Company. They went on to New Orleans for the Mardi Gras. (They approached New Orleans in a thunderstorm and the Sikorsky's left engine suddenly quit. Hughes brought the aircraft to a landing on the Mississippi River, some thirty miles from New Orleans. A coast guard vessel towed the amphibian into New Orleans where Odekirk repaired the faulty engine.) Ten days later, the duo flew to Richmond, Virginia, where Hughes competed in a golf tournament. Next stop was the Sikorsky plant in Bridgeport, Connecticut. The pair spent the summer in the New York area. At the end of the summer, Hughes left "Odie" to work on the plane while he went to Europe.

During a visit to Europe in 1933, Hughes purchased the luxurious steam yacht, "Rover," renaming it "Southern Cross." The yacht's elegant accommodations and size made it a miniature ocean liner, and the fifth largest private yacht in the world.

Before returning to the states, Hughes bought a steam yacht, *Rover,* a 286-foot British twin-screw vessel. He renamed it *Southern Cross.* Manned by a crew of thirty, it was the fifth largest private yacht in the world. Hughes returned to New York near the start of winter, 1933, and told Odekirk to get the Sikorsky ready to fly to Miami. Hughes decided to enter the Boeing 100A in the All-American Air Meet.

On January 14, 1934, Hughes flew the Boeing to an easy victory in the Sportsman Pilot Free-For-All at the Miami All-American Air Meet. The racer was so fast that it nearly lapped its closest competitor. Hughes was elated over his victory, but he still was not satisfied with the performance of the Boeing. He wanted more speed. Finally, an exasperated Odekirk told Hughes that if he wanted a faster airplane, he would have to design it himself.

In total secrecy, Hughes began work on what the press quickly dubbed the "Hughes Mystery Ship." Hughes referred to his design as the H-1 (Hughes, First Design) and gathered an impressive team of talented engineers and mechanics. Foremost among them was Dick Palmer, a recent graduate of Caltech who was already noted for his radical ideas about aircraft design.

Hughes was personally involved in every facet of the H-1's design and construction. He was determined to incorporate the latest advances in aviation technology into a sleek racing machine. He was going to build a plane that was far superior to anything ever before built. To this end, he spared no expense. With Hughes' ability to provide the design team with every necessary resource, it took only eighteen months to complete the racer.

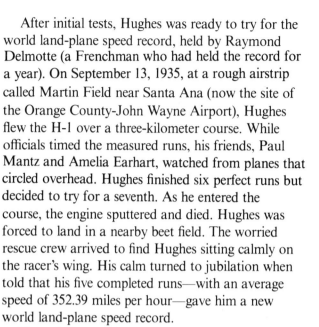

The H-1 was rolled out for public inspection on August 18, 1935. Onlookers gasped in awe. At a time when biplanes had open cockpits, fixed landing gear and wings braced with struts and wires, the H-1 looked foreign. It had a single cantilevered wing and tail and no external struts or braces. It was powered by a compact 1,535-cubic-inch Pratt and Whitney *Wasp, Jr.,* radial engine beefed up to 1,000 horsepower. The engine cowl was formfitted around the engine, reducing airstream drag to a minimum. The fuselage was composed of riveted, polished aluminum. Each rivet had been countersunk and was flush with the surface of the skin—the first time that flush rivets were used on an airplane. While most airplanes of the time used fixed landing gear, the racer had mechanically-operated retractable gear.

The racer—built specifically for speed— incorporated every technological advance that Hughes and his engineers could build into it. One associate said the only way it could have achieved one extra mile per hour in speed was if Hughes himself were a smaller pilot: the plane's cockpit was formfit around Hughes' six-foot-three-inch frame.

Hughes personally conducted the flight test of the H-1, as he did with all of his future airplane designs. When asked why he didn't hire a test pilot to handle this dangerous task, Hughes answered, "Hell, why should I pay somebody else to have all the fun?"

After initial tests, Hughes was ready to try for the world land-plane speed record, held by Raymond Delmotte (a Frenchman who had held the record for a year). On September 13, 1935, at a rough airstrip called Martin Field near Santa Ana (now the site of the Orange County-John Wayne Airport), Hughes flew the H-1 over a three-kilometer course. While officials timed the measured runs, his friends, Paul Mantz and Amelia Earhart, watched from planes that circled overhead. Hughes finished six perfect runs but decided to try for a seventh. As he entered the course, the engine sputtered and died. Hughes was forced to land in a nearby beet field. The worried rescue crew arrived to find Hughes sitting calmly on the racer's wing. His calm turned to jubilation when told that his five completed runs—with an average speed of 352.39 miles per hour—gave him a new world land-plane speed record.

The aviation world was suddenly forced to take Howard Hughes seriously. The H-1 was a revolutionary airplane and it would influence aircraft design for decades. In fact, the H-1 now hangs in its own alcove in the Smithsonian's National Air and Space Museum in Washington, D.C.

With Hughes at the controls, the H-1 racer, dubbed the "zoinged bullet" by the press, roars aloft from the Santa Ana, California, airport; 1935.

Hughes made his mark with this plane and his speed record, but he immediately wanted to challenge the transcontinental speed record. It would take time to repair his racer, however, so the impatient Hughes acquired a new plane, a Northrop Gamma, from the famous woman pilot Jackie Cochran. He modified it for the cross-country hop. Hughes' team replaced the Gamma's engine with a new Wright Cyclone R-1820G capable of 925 horsepower.

Hughes took off from Burbank, California, on January 13, 1936, for what he claimed was a "test run" to check the course. Just nine hours and twenty-seven minutes later, he landed in Newark, New Jersey, with a new record. After landing, a casual Hughes told reporters, "I wanted to go to New York, so I tried to see how fast I could do it." But there was more to Hughes' impromptu flight than just a fast joyride: he used the flight to check fuel consumption and speed at high altitudes; he also proved his theory that flight instruments calibrated at sea level are not accurate at high altitudes. And, he used this as a test run for his next flight—the transcontinental run using his own H-1.

Hughes retraces the route of his 1936 trans-continental flight in the Northrup Gamma while relaxing at the Waldorf-Astoria in New York City.

(Below) Hughes with H-1 racer shortly after wheels-up landing in a beet field near Santa Ana, California. A clogged fuel line was reported to have caused the accident. Hughes was uninjured and the plane only slightly damaged.

After the transcontinental flight in the Gamma, Hughes made several other flights before returning to Los Angeles. Each time the Gamma touched down at a new city, Hughes had established another point-to-point speed record. On April 26, 1936, he flew from Miami to New York, covering the 1,196-mile distance in four hours and twenty-two minutes with an average speed of 276 miles per hour—a new record for this run. On his trip back to California, he broke the Chicago-to-Los Angeles speed record.

Hughes suddenly was a renowned aviator, with three major speed records to his name. But he was still not satisfied. He knew his H-1 could easily break the records he had just set with the Gamma. He ordered the racer prepared for a special flight. The H-1 was refitted with a boosted engine and a longer set of wings, measuring thirty-two feet, nine inches, which were best for long distance, high altitude flights. While the racer was being prepared, Hughes was awarded the prestigious Harmon Trophy for his record-breaking transcontinental flights in the Gamma. Hughes planned to accept the trophy in grand style.

On January 19, 1937, en route to receive his trophy, Hughes flew the modified H-1, now appropriately dubbed the "Winged Bullet," from Los Angeles to Newark in seven hours, twenty-eight minutes and thirty-five seconds. He had cut two hours off his own record. The racer averaged a speed of 332 miles per hour over the 2,490-mile course, a record which stood for the next seven years.

Hughes immediately planned his next aviation goal, an ambitious one indeed. He wanted to re-create pilot Wiley Post's around-the-world flight, but not in a daredevil stunt fashion. Hughes wanted to demonstrate the efficiency, reliability, and speed of America's modern transport aircraft. Only a few hardy souls in the United States had ever flown in an airplane, and Hughes wanted to change the public's opinion about this up-and-coming industry.

He planned this venture with characteristic thoroughness. After two years of careful preparation—in which he conducted a detailed study of all available airplanes, comparing their speed and performance data—Hughes felt he was ready. He selected a twin-engine Lockheed Model 14 *Lodestar* for the trip because of its superior speed.

Hughes packed the aircraft with the latest in aviation equipment: sophisticated communications and navigational gear; instruments that allowed for automatic and blind flying; even the new Sperry Gyro

Hughes at Grand Central Airport, Glendale, California; August 26, 1939.

Pilot to maintain level flight automatically. And to provide accurate weather information to his aircraft while en route, Hughes established a global communications network. (This system predated and helped establish the national weather service that now performs the same function for pilots today.)

Hughes' preparations were so thorough that special fuel stations were set up at scheduled landing fields as well. And, in case engine failure forced him to ditch the airplane at sea, Hughes was determined to make the airplane unsinkable. He ordered his crew to find a light buoyant substance with which to fill empty spaces in the wings and fuselage. Their ideal solution: Ping Pong balls. Eighty pounds were used for flotation aboard the *Lockheed-14*.

Hughes chose four outstanding aviators to accompany him: Harry P. McLean Conner, copilot-navigator; Thomas Thurlow, primary navigator; Richard Stoddard, radioman; and Ed Lund, flight engineer.

On the afternoon of July 10, 1938, Hughes and his crew were ready. The Lockheed-14 was christened *The New York World's Fair 1939*—to promote Hughes' desire for world unity. Hughes was asked to say a few words before he boarded his airplane. He told reporters and well-wishers, "We hope that our flight may prove a contribution to the cause of friendship between nations and that through their outstanding fliers, for whom the common bond of

aviation transcends national boundaries, this cause may be furthered."

Hughes climbed aboard and taxied his plane to the end of the runway. As Hughes applied power, the fully-loaded aircraft responded sluggishly; it picked up speed slowly. As the plane approached the end of the paved runway, it was still firmly on the ground. The worried spectators watched as the plane suddenly ran off the paved runway and into the dirt. A cloud of dust engulfed it. Then, rising slowly above the dust, the *Lockheed-14* appeared and began to climb skyward. The crowd burst into enthusiastic cheers.

The first leg of the trip was the New York-to-Paris run. Hughes wanted to break the existing speed record set by Charles Lindbergh during his solo hop in 1927. When Hughes landed at Le Bourget Airport, he learned that he had not only broken Lindbergh's record, but he had actually cut it in half. Hughes and his crew had landed in France only sixteen hours and thirty-eight minutes after leaving New York.

In Paris, Hughes was delayed for eight hours while a damaged landing strut was repaired. Hughes then flew to Moscow and refueled, with additional refueling stops scheduled for Omsk, Yakutsk (cities in the Soviet Union), Fairbanks, and finally Minneapolis.

(Above) Hughes' Sikorsky S-38 amphibian, pictured in 1932, was considered for the around-the-world flight, but rejected in favor of the Lockheed 14.

(Below) The Lockheed 14 is surrounded by 1,000 police and a crowd of 30,000 well-wishers after its arrival in New York City.

A bearded and happy Hughes leaves Floyd Bennet Field with New York Mayor Fiorello La Guardia, 1939 World's Fair Director Grover Whalen, and flight coordinator Albert Lodwick, following his arrival from the around-the-world flight.

As they left Yakutsk, Hughes and his crew encountered a nasty surprise: a range of mountains considerably higher than indicated on their charts. Hughes quickly put the *Lodestar* into a climb and barely cleared the tops of the 9,700-foot-high jagged peaks. (If Hughes had flown this leg at night, he would have smashed into the side of the rugged peaks.)

When Hughes landed in Fairbanks, Alaska, at 8:18 P.M., on July 13, he was greeted by Wiley Post's widow, who wished them luck. After a record pit stop in Minneapolis (just thirty-four minutes), they roared into the air on their last leg—to New York. Bad weather plagued them but Hughes guided the *Lodestar* down through the clouds for a smooth landing at Floyd Bennett Field. Hughes had established a new world record: circumnavigation of the globe in just ninety-one hours.

As the *Lodestar* rolled to a stop, thousands of exuberant spectators broke through police barricades and swarmed around the aircraft. Hughes and his crew were surrounded by the cheering, shoving throng. Finally, police managed to escort Hughes to the microphone platform where Grover Whalen and New York Mayor Fiorello H. La Guardia waited. The Mayor's welcome was brief: "Seven million New Yorkers offer congratulations for the greatest record established in the history of aviation." A modest Hughes commented, "If credit is due anyone, it is due to the men who designed and perfected to its present remarkable state of efficiency the modern American flying machine and equipment. If we made a fast flight, it is because so many young men in this country went to engineering schools, worked hard at drafting tables and designed a fast airplane and navigation and radio equipment which would keep this plane upon its course. All we did was operate this equipment and

plane according to the instruction book accompanying the article."

The around-the-world flight elevated Hughes to worldwide prominence. A ticker tape parade down Broadway was given to Hughes by proud New Yorkers. He was overwhelmed with awards, again winning the coveted Harmon Trophy, which was presented by President Franklin D. Roosevelt. He received the Collier Trophy, the Octave Chanute Award, a Congressional Medal and hundreds of other awards and citations.

Hughes, always impatient to move on, began to plan a second world flight. This was to be a goodwill tour of world capitals. He wanted to fly the new Boeing Model 307 *Stratoliner,* the first pressurized, high-altitude aircraft. He intended to prove that reliable, comfortable and safe commercial transportation was a reality.

These lofty plans were canceled because of the war in Europe.

(Below) Hughes, in his leather flight helmet, waits while the ground crew inspects the H-1 prior to flight.

(Opposite, above) The crew prepares to remove the H-1 from the beet field after its forced landing.

(Opposite, below) H-1 in storage at Newark Airport, New Jersey, following its trans-Atlantic flight in 1937.

(Above) A confident Hughes poses in cockpit of
Northrup Gamma in which he set his transcontinental
speed record in 1936.

(Inset) Hughes at dinner in Los Angeles after record
flight in N-6 from Illinois to Los Angeles; May 14, 1936.

(Above) Northrup Gamma, acquired from aviatrix Jackie Cochran, sits outside terminal at Floyd Bennet Field in New York.

(Below) Hughes, sporting his trademark fedora, and flight crew meet the press before around-the-world flight. (Left to right) Ed Lund, Hughes, Grover Whalen (director of the 1939 World's Fair), Harry Connor, Richard Stoddart, and Lt. Thomas Thurlow.

(Above) Hughes and crew land in Paris with new trans-Atlantic crossing time of 16 hours and 38 minutes; first leg of the round-the-world flight.

(Left) Hughes checks the damaged tail of his Lockheed 14 in Paris.

(Below) Hughes is greeted by the Soviet Ambassador to the United States, A. Toryanovski, during a refueling stop in Moscow.

(Opposite, above) This map charts Hughes' progress during his world flight. Stops included Omsk and Yakutsk in the USSR and Fairbanks, Alaska.

(Above) Fairbanks, Alaska, airport from the air.
(Inset) During a fuel stop in Fairbanks, Hughes and his
crew were greeted by the widow of Wiley Post, whose
speed record Hughes was attempting to beat.
Next stop: Minneapolis, Minnesota.

(Above) The Lockheed 14 races for New York City.

(Inset) Newspapers around the world followed the exploits of Hughes and his crew as they raced from city to city. This is from the Cleveland Press, *July 14, 1938.*

(Below) Aerial photograph of Floyd Bennet Field shows 30,000 spectators and 1,000 police jamming the terminal area waiting to welcome Hughes and his crew.
(Opposite) Motorcycles, crowds, and the press throng the Floyd Bennet airfield as Hughes pilots his award-winning Lockheed 14 into the terminal.

(Opposite) Hughes walks across the lobby of the Waldorf-Astoria Hotel, complete with admiring bellhop, on his way to the ticker-tape parade down Broadway.

(Above) Hughes and flight crew appear with Mayor La Guardia on the steps of New York's City Hall.

(Left) Chicago ticker-tape parade on La Salle Street, July 20, 1938.

75

(Opposite) Hughes visits Houston
plant of Hughes Tool Company and
chats with workers on July 30, 1938.

(Above) Hughes, feted at a Houston
dinner in honor of his world flight, is
seated with Noah Dietrich, his public
relations manager and advisor.

(Below) Hughes Tool Company
employees give "the boss" a warm
welcome.

Hughes prepares for the first test flight of the second version of XF-11 photo reconnaissance plane on April 5, 1947.

PART FOUR:

The War Years

Germany's attack on Poland in 1939 was a stunning blow to complacent military leaders around the world. The fury and success of Hitler's Blitzkrieg, or "lightning war," was astonishing. The world has never seen a military force as powerful as this, and the key ingredient was its air power. The U.S. Army Air Corps, with its antiquated airplanes, kept a worried eye on the European war. If called upon to fight, its air force would be outclassed and outnumbered. Multimillion dollar contracts were awarded to major aircraft manufacturers to develop fighters, bombers, and cargo aircraft that would be able to compete with those of the Germans.

Howard Hughes was determined to stay in the vanguard of aeronautical development. For years he had spoken of his concern that America was lagging behind Europe in aviation technology. Now his patriotic zeal was sparked. He was determined to help the war effort by building a superior military aircraft.

Contracts for aircraft development were primarily controlled by the U.S. Army Air Corps through its test, research and development installation at Wright Field near Dayton, Ohio. Twice before the outbreak of the war, Hughes had vainly tried to land contracts with Wright Field officials. In 1937, when the H-1 held almost every major speed record in the country, Hughes wanted to sell the design to the government for use as a pursuit fighter. But the Wright Field generals were not interested: the aircraft was not built to government specifications. Hughes believed he was not treated fairly. True, his unorthodox methods sometimes irked government officials, but whatever the reason, the H-1 was rejected for military use.

Ironically, one of the most successful fighters in World War II, the deadly Japanese Zero, closely resembled the H-1 in design. Several groups of Japanese officials had inspected and photographed the H-1 during its public displays. Many, including Hughes, were convinced that the Zero utilized the same basic design as the H-1, although some aviation historians disagree. However, Hughes firmly believed

that his design was copied and was forever bitter toward the American military leaders who rejected the H-1 in 1937.

Hughes made a second attempt to land a military contract later that year. He presented a design for a fast twin-engine fighter, but Lockheed won the contract to build a similar airplane, which became one of our most successful fighters, the brawny P-38 Lightning. In this case, Hughes simply lost to a superior design.

Undaunted, Hughes decided to build an airplane so superior to all others that Wright Field would be unable to ignore it. Dubbed the D-2 (for Design Number Two), the aircraft was designed as a fast, high-flying bomber that could carry a crew of five. Hughes, once again going against prescribed guidelines for military aircraft, built the D-2 out of wood. He investigated a special process called

Hughes discusses engineering details on D-2 bomber at the Culver City, California, plant on July 4, 1943.

Hughes inspects engines for his wooden D-2 bomber prototype.

Duramold, developed by the Fairchild Corporation. It was a revolutionary system of composite laminate bonding that placed thin veneers of wood between layers of specially formulated glues. Sherman Fairchild and Hughes were good friends and both believed that the Duramold system would produce a strong, light structure ideally suited for an airplane. The smooth glasslike finish would greatly reduce drag, increasing the aircraft's speed.

Hughes purchased a tract of land in Culver City, California, to serve as headquarters for his growing Hughes Aircraft Company. He built a 9,000-foot runway for aircraft testing and constructed several large buildings to house the design and production facilities. Working almost exclusively on the D-2 project, Hughes and his engineers encountered numerous problems. Since the D-2 was low on the Air Force's priority list, they had trouble obtaining the materials needed to build the prototype. When

Hughes could not get the type of engines he needed, he was forced to change the design from a bomber to a smaller twin-engine fighter. In spite of these problems, Hughes pressed on.

As usual, he insisted on total secrecy during the D-2's construction. One day a party of top military officials, including General H. H. (Hap) Arnold, the commander of the Air Force, arrived to inspect the D-2. Security guards did not allow them to enter without Hughes' approval and Hughes was unavailable. The party left, furious.

Even before the prototype was finished, the military informed Hughes that the D-2 did not suit their requirements; they were not interested in a wooden airplane. They felt that metal construction was far superior. Hughes did succeed in bringing his design to the attention of Major General Oliver P. Echols, the Air Force procurement officer, who finally ordered his staff to evaluate the plane. After

studying the plane, however, the Wright Field engineers concluded that it did not qualify, under their standards, as military aircraft because of its wooden construction. Hughes still refused to concede and continued the project on his own.

While he continued the D-2's development, Hughes joined forces with Henry Kaiser in 1942 to build a giant cargo flying boat. He divided his time among these two projects and his other business and filmmaking enterprises.

On June 20, 1943, the finished D-2 prototype was ready for a test flight, to be held at Harper Dry Lake in the Mojave Desert. Hughes was not pleased with the plane after the test flight; once again, a plane did not live up to his expectations. He ordered major modifications in its design. But on the night of November 11, 1943, the D-2 hangar caught fire. The aircraft was totally destroyed. Lightning was later blamed for the accident.

Determined to continue the ill-fated project, Hughes began development of the D-5, a larger, more sophisticated version of the D-2. This new plane would have two Pratt and Whitney Wasp Major engines, the most powerful aircraft engines available. By using these large engines, Hughes hoped to build an airplane with the speed of a fighter and the long range of a bomber.

Hughes pushed himself to the breaking point,

(Above) Following the crash of the first XF-11 model, Hughes successfully test flew this second version of the XF-11 after recovering from his crash injuries. This version has single propellers on each engine.

(Below) Hughes reviews plans for his Culver City plant in 1947 with top engineers.

working simultaneously on the D-5 and the Flying Boat. He spent his daylight hours with his engineers on the aircraft projects and his night hours on his other business ventures.

Hughes once again tried to interest government officials in his D-5, but they remained aloof. They felt that the D-2 had performed poorly on its test flight and that the D-5 was merely a reworked D-2.

Just as the D-5 project seemed doomed, Hughes received a boost from an influential source. Colonel Elliott Roosevelt, the president's son, had become an expert on strategic photo-reconnaisance and was displeased with the quality of the Air Force's photo-reconnaisance aircraft. Since successful photo-reconnaisance was vital to the success of the war effort and U.S. planes were being lost in great numbers due to the superiority of the Italian and German aircraft, it was imperative that a first class airplane be developed. It had to fly higher and faster than any enemy pursuit ships and it had to be capable of dashing behind enemy lines and returning with critical photographs.

In June 1943, Roosevelt, under orders from General Hap Arnold, toured aircraft plants across the country, scouting for suitable photo-reconnaissance aircraft. Hughes saw this as an opportunity to save his cherished D-5 project; he met with Roosevelt and spent hours showing him drawings and specifications. Hughes believed that with minor modifications, the D-5 would make an ideal high-speed, high-altitude aircraft. Roosevelt was impressed with the D-5 and with Hughes and his staff of experienced engineers.

He returned to Washington, D.C., and recommended that the Army order photo-reconnaissance airplanes from the Hughes Aircraft Company. In late 1943, Hughes was awarded a contract to develop his design. It was designated the XF-11 and would be of metal construction. The contract called for three prototypes and ninety-seven production models. Hughes was elated.

Unfortunately, neither the XF-11 nor the Flying Boat was completed in time to contribute to the war effort. The Allies, aided by America's vast industrial strength, were wearing down the Nazi war machine. Hughes, with typical determination, continued his aircraft projects. He was certain they would still be needed in the postwar world.

Although Hughes never realized his dream of producing a military aircraft for war service, his various companies did contribute substantially to the war effort. At the Culver City plant, the Hughes Aircraft Company patented and produced the "flexible feed chute," which speeded the loading of machine guns on American bombers. The company also produced special electric booster drives that reduced machine gun jamming. And they manufactured various wing panels for parts for military planes. The Hughes Tool Company in Houston produced parts for B-25 and B-26 bombers; the Tool Company also managed the Dickson Gun Plant, which manufactured gun barrels. While Hughes never succeeded in producing a military airplane for wartime use, his contributions to the war effort were invaluable.

The Sikorsky S-43 is hauled from the bottom of Lake Mead in Nevada. The plane had crashed with Hughes at the controls, killing two crewmen. The May 29, 1943, test flight was for the U.S. Army Corps of Engineers, to whom Hughes was selling the Sikorsky.

To
Elai J. Gmar -
Your past pindness and
cooperation is truly appreciated.
I hope that some day Long Beach
will regard this plane with a certain
amount of pride.
Howard Hughes

The Hughes Flying Boat on its surprise flight, November 2, 1947, at Long Beach, California.

The Hughes Flying Boat—
"Spruce Goose"

The first notion for Howard Hughes' Flying Boat, the legendary "Spruce Goose," belonged to Henry J. Kaiser, the brilliant steel magnate and shipbuilder. During World War II, Kaiser's shipyards built small freighters ("Liberty Ships") at an incredibly fast rate. But Nazi submarines on the North Atlantic sank them as quickly as they were built. In July 1942, 800,000 tons of Allied shipping were sunk. England was unable to receive adequate supplies from Canada and the United States and was near collapse. During those dark days, Kaiser had a flash of brilliance: Why not put wings on his Liberty Ships? They would be able to fly over the submarines and land on any large stretch of water. Kaiser quickly outlined a proposal to build a fleet of 5,000 giant twin-hulled flying boats, each one large enough to carry hundreds of troops, tons of supplies, or a 60-ton Sherman tank. But when

Kaiser sought government funding to proceed with his plan, he found resistance. Top military officials conceded that Kaiser was a shipbuilding genius, but they did not think he had sufficient aeronautical expertise to take on such a huge project. Aviation experts across the country said that such an airplane—to be larger than anything in existence— was impossible. Besides, shortages of strategic materials such as steel and aluminum precluded the construction of such a fleet of flying boats.

Kaiser, unruffled by the rejection, set out to find the aviation expertise he needed. He found it in Howard Hughes. Hughes' recent aviation exploits made him a national hero and he was a proven pilot, a brilliant technician, and a revolutionary aircraft designer.

At first Hughes was not interested in the idea of

building a giant cargo plane. He preferred fast, maneuverable bombers and fighters. But when Kaiser told Hughes that the consensus among aircraft designers was that the task was impossible, Hughes' interested was piqued. He finally yielded to Kaiser's persuasive sales pitch and to his own competitive nature. The two men joined forces to design and construct the giant flying boat.

Together they formed the Kaiser-Hughes Corporation and on November 16, 1942—a year after Pearl Harbor—they received an $18 million contract for three prototype flying boats: two flying models and one static test model. The contract stated that neither Hughes nor Kaiser would receive any profit from the project. The most demanding clause stated that the project could not utilize two strategic metals, steel and aluminum, which were in short supply.

Hughes and Kaiser were convinced that they could build the flying boats out of wood, using the Duramold system. The Duramold process—a technique of bonding thin layers of wood veneer with special glues—had been leased from the Fairchild Corporation and was further developed by Hughes Aircraft engineers. Hughes perfected the process to the point where it was a suitable material for aircraft construction, but adapting the process to a project of this size would be a major engineering endeavor.

Hughes shocked the aviation community as he unveiled his preliminary plans. The proposed aircraft was even larger than the one described by Kaiser: it would have a gross weight of 400,000 pounds (200 tons) and a wingspan of 320 feet. (This was nearly six times larger than any existing aircraft.) Aviation experts claimed that the very idea of such an aircraft was ludicrous; nothing that big could even fly!

Hughes ignored his critics and began work on the HK-1 (Hughes-Kaiser, First Design) at his Culver City plant. The project was plagued with problems from the beginning. First, and most important, the flying boat was low on the military's priority list for construction materials. Second, complex jigs and special equipment were needed to fabricate the various Duramold components of the aircraft. Hughes' own eccentric working style caused delays as well. In addition, the Hughes Aircraft Company had to build a larger structure to house the project. It became the largest wooden building ever built—750 feet long, 250 feet wide and 100 feet high.

As work continued through 1943 and into 1944, the severity of the initial U-boat menace diminished.

(Above, opposite) The Spruce Goose under construction in Culver City; 1946.

(Above) Flying Boar sections ready for assembly in Long Beach harbor drydock following the two-day, 28-mile trip from the Culver City plant.

(Opposite) On June 15-16, 1946, dozens of police motorcycles escort fuselage along city streets during the 28-mile trek.

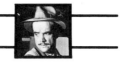

The Allied armies and navies were wreaking havoc on the Nazi forces and it became clear that a fleet of giant transport aircraft would not be needed to win the war.

The government took steps to eliminate the Kaiser-Hughes contract. Hughes insisted that their Flying Boat was a valuable research and development project. The government finally agreed to allow Hughes to finish the one craft currently under construction. When the $18 million from the original agreement was exhausted, Hughes personally invested more than $7 million to finish the project.

By 1946, it was nearing completion and Hughes searched for a waterfront location for the final assembly and eventual flight test. A suitable spot was leased on Terminal Island in Long Beach Harbor. Assembly commenced on a 290-foot-long graving dock. The dry dock was needed to launch the aircraft and to allow the wings to be attached with the hull below ground level.

In June 1946, the monumental task of moving the Flying Boat from Culver City to Long Beach began. The Star House Movers of Long Beach were hired at a cost of $80,000. The move took two days, with the enormous wing sections resting overnight in a field. As the huge fuselage moved down the city's streets, schools along the route recessed for the day so children could watch the plane's progress. Highway engineers checked roadways and bridges along the route to be sure they would not crumble under the boat's weight. The police forces of ten cities and municipalities guarded the aircraft as it moved towards Long Beach. The electric and phone companies sent linemen to cut down thousands of electrical lines before the procession arrived and to splice them back after the aircraft passed by. Tree trimmers made sure no trees or shrubs obstructed the Flying Boat's path.

After it crossed the old pontoon bridge linking Terminal Island with downtown Long Beach, the Hughes Flying Boat finally arrived at the harbor facilities. Engineers began the difficult task of lowering the fuselage down into the twenty-foot-deep dry dock. With the fuselage secure on cribbing blocks in the bottom of the graving dock, workmen attached the wing, tail and control components of the aircraft. As this work progressed, Hughes returned to Culver City to begin the final flight testing of his cherished XF-11.

Construction on the XF-11 had continued through 1944 and 1945. The first prototype was finally ready

The contra-rotating propellers of the first XF-11 are clearly seen in this photo taken moments before Hughes began the test flight that ended in disaster.

(Opposite) When one of the propellers malfunctioned, Hughes crashed into a residential area of Beverly Hills on July 5, 1946.

for testing in the summer of 1946. On July 7, 1946, just one month after he moved the Flying Boat to conduct the first actual flight test of the XF-11. Hughes, who always test piloted the airplanes he designed, climbed into the cockpit of the bullet-nosed machine.

He nestled into the narrow pilot's seat and fired up the powerful engines, Pratt and Whitney R-4360's, the same engines that were being installed on the Hughes Flying Boat. (They are the largest piston-driven engines ever designed for aircraft, producing 3,000 horsepower each.) After a careful check of the engines and of the electrical and mechanical systems, Hughes began a series of taxi tests. Reassured that everything was working perfectly, he guided the craft to the end of the 9,000-foot runway.

He signaled to his ground crew and to the observation plane that circled overhead, then opened the throttle to full power. The XF-11 shot forward. He pulled back on the stick and lifted the airplane into the air, retracting its landing gear. Although Hughes felt the gear thump into their bays, a red warning light on the panel indicated a malfunction of the gear mechanism. Hughes tried to determine the nature of the problem by lowering and retracting the landing gear, but the red light remained lit. Finally, he put the gear down and retracted them while pushing forward on the aircraft's control yoke, adding G-force to the wheels as they folded into their bays. The red light blinked out. Hughes went through a series of flight test procedures as he circled over the Los

Angeles area for about forty-five minutes. He had just turned the XF-11 towards his Culver City base when disaster struck.

To Hughes, it felt as if a giant fist had slammed into the right wing of the airplane. The nose pitched down and the XF-11 fell into a spiral dive. He remembered the gear warning light and surmised that a gear door had come open and was twisted broadside to the airflow. He quickly cycled and recycled the landing gear with no effect. As the struggling aircraft lost altitude, Hughes attempted to regain control of the XF-11, but to no avail. Over a populated area and too low to bail out, he tried desperately to keep the ship in the air long enough to reach the Los Angeles Country Club, only a few miles away, but he never made it.

The XF-11 crashed through the roof of a house on Wilshire Boulevard. Its momentum hurled it between two more houses. Both wings were clipped off while the fuselage and cockpit slammed to earth and slid to a stop in an alley. The plane's ruptured fuel tanks exploded in a violent, deafening blast and sent skyward a ball of flames and dense black smoke.

A Marine sergeant visiting friends nearby heard the explosion and rushed to the crash site. Sergeant William Durkin was almost certain that no one could have survived such an inferno, but he wasted no time in crawling through the flames on his hands and knees to investigate. He was about to give up his search when he heard a loud thud. A badly injured Hughes had pulled himself from the shattered fuselage and

collapsed onto the broken wing of the aircraft. As Durkin got closer, Hughes rolled onto the ground, unconscious. Durkin braved the fire and rushed to Hughes' side and pulled him to safety.

Hughes was rushed to the hospital in critical condition and a team of doctors agreed it would be a miracle if he survived the night. He was in severe shock; he had suffered a crushed chest; every rib was cracked or broken; his heart was dislocated; his clavicle and nose were fractured; he had suffered deep wounds on the scalp, extensive second- and third-degree burns, and numerous cuts and abrasions; one lung had collapsed and the other was damaged.

Hughes not only survived the night, but he also walked out of the hospital after only five weeks. (As he recuperated, the irascible Hughes was annoyed at having to lie flat on his back in an uncomfortable hospital bed. He especially disliked having to use the necessary bedpan. Hughes demanded pencil and paper and quickly sketched plans for a mechanically adjustable hospital bed that featured numerous position settings for maximum patient comfort and even a remote-controlled retractable bedpan. Hughes engineers built the bed at the Culver City plant and delivered it to the hospital, but apparently Hughes

recovered before actually using it.)

Hughes went back to work immediately and conducted a complete reevaluation of the problems that caused the XF-11 crash. Many of Hughes' detractors tried to blame the crash on his piloting inabilities. Hughes was determined to clear his record.

The cause of the crash was determined to be a leak in a hydraulic seal governing the variable pitch on the right-hand set of propellers: one of the contra-rotating props had gone into full reverse pitch and had pushed backwards on the right side of the airplane. The prop failure made Hughes wary of the contra-rotating propeller system; the second XF-11 prototype utilized single props on each of its two engines.

On April 5, 1947, Hughes successfully test flew the revised XF-11 and turned it over to the military. But since the war was over, the government no longer

needed a fleet of reconnaissance aircraft. Hughes built only those two XF-11 airplanes.

After convalescing from his accident, Hughes was ready to test the Flying Boat. His determination to test the airplane was further prompted by a series of investigations by a Senate subcommittee: political foes were trying to prove that Hughes had profited from his wartime contracts. Of course, just the opposite was true. Hughes had contributed much of his own money to these projects; in fact, he had personally invested more than $7 million to complete the Hughes Flying Boat alone.

During the Senate hearings in Washington, D.C., Hughes was accused of building a flying lumberyard, a "spruce goose" that he knew would never fly. An outraged Hughes stated that he had done what he thought was right for the war effort: "I put the sweat of my life" into the Flying Boat. Finally the angry Hughes told the senators that if the Flying Boat failed, he would "probably leave this country and never come back." Hughes returned to California and prepared the seaplane for taxi tests.

The aircraft was launched on November 1, 1947, but high winds and rough seas prevented any tests. The next morning dawned bright and clear. A strong steady breeze kicked up small whitecaps in Long Beach's outer harbor, and Hughes decided to proceed with the tests. He boarded the Flying Boat and supervised as the airplane was towed by sea to the first taxi test of this mighty airship. Speculation raged over whether Hughes would try to fly the aircraft. Most observers felt he would not try a flight until he had conducted extensive surface tests. Hughes himself said, "No flight test will be attempted until April of 1948."

Hughes took his place in the left seat of the Flying Boat, wearing his famous brown fedora. He was accompanied by eighteen crewmen, five company officials and nine special guests. Only the copilot, Dave Grant, was chosen personally by Hughes, and, surprisingly enough, Grant was not a pilot. He was the hydraulic engineer who had designed and supervised the installation of the powerful system. Many observers felt that Hughes chose Grant so that there

(Opposite) Hughes appeared before a Senate investigating committee on August 11, 1947, to defend the huge flying boat, nicknamed "The Spruce Goose" by its detractors. (Below) Hughes confronts chairman Senator Homer Ferguson while Senator Owen Brewster (standing) looks on.

(Below) July 1946: The nearly complete Flying Boat awaits installation and final assembly of its propellers in the Long Beach Harbor drydock.

Hughes poses with his Spruce Goose crew on November 1, 1947—the day before the successful flight. Some members of the crew include: Dave Grant (third from left), Glenn Odekirk (on Hughes' left), Ray Hopper (second from Hughes' right), and Bill Beary (third from right).

would be absolutely no doubt that Hughes alone piloted the craft. Perhaps; but more than likely, Hughes was concerned about the operation of the hydraulic system. It was vital to the success of the tests, and in the event of a problem, Hughes wanted the man most knowledgeable about the system sitting next to him. Besides, Hughes seldom used a copilot, even on his multi-engine aircraft, and in any case the Hughes Flying Boat was not scheduled to fly on this day.

The other sixteen crew positions were coveted by everyone involved in the project. The crew chief, Chuck Jucker, made the final selections: Joe Petralli and Donald Smith, flight engineers; Warren Read, assistant chief engineer; Dave Evans, radio operator; Merle Coffee and Jack Jacobson, electricians: Thomas Dugdale and Bill Noggle, hydraulic mechanics; Phillip Thibodeau, Harry Kaiser, Al Gererink, Jim Thompson, Donald Shirey, John Glenn, Mel Glaser, and Dave Van Storm, aircraft mechanics.

In addition to the crew, several officials were aboard for the tests: George Haldeman, CAA representative; Mathew Whelan, Pratt and Whitney representative; Bill Newman, Hughes Company photographer; Rea Hopper, William Berry, Dave Roe, and Jim Dallas, Hughes Aircraft Company engineering representatives.

Hughes provided a few seats for representatives of the press, who were selected by a lottery system. The winners: Jim Padgett, International News Service; Joe Johnson, newsreel pool photographer, and his assistant, Dexter Alley; Ralph Dighton, Associated Press; John Vonderheide, United Press International; and James McNamara, radio pool announcer (accompanied by his recording engineer). The reporters left behind were reduced to pushing and shoving for position on the press boats Hughes provided.

Dozens of pleasure craft swarmed around the outer harbor while Coast Guard vessels darted about, trying to keep them clear of the massive Flying Boat. Thousands of spectators crammed every available spot along the shoreline piers, jetties and even the naval vessels at the Long Beach Naval Shipyard. Rainbow Pier, jutting out in a graceful arc from downtown Long Beach, was packed with autos and pedestrians.

On the flight deck, Hughes settled into his seat, nearly thirty feet above the water, removed his brown fedora, and put on his earphones. After last-minute

checks on the controls, Hughes fired up the eight massive engines one by one. He gradually opened the throttles; the Flying Boat moved away from the Long Beach skyline toward the San Pedro end of the breakwater. As the boat picked up speed, the choppy waves beat a deafening rhythm against the ship's hull. The sound of the waves echoed through the empty cargo deck. The Flying Boat traveled about thirty-five miles per hour on this first run as Hughes tested the various controls.

(One interesting but overlooked item is that the Spruce Goose had only four throttles at the time of the flight, even though it had eight engines. The original configuration linked two engines in tandem to each throttle. Hughes found this unacceptable. After docking the boat, he ordered the hydro-pneumatic throttle linkage to be changed to an electro-mechanical system with one throttle for each engine.)

After the first slow-speed run, Hughes turned to the passengers and told them to hold on because he was going to "...really pick up some speed on this run." Smoothly and rapidly, Hughes advanced the throttles and the giant seaplane accelerated. It skipped gracefully across the waves at nearly ninety miles per hours. The forward portion of the hull was clear of the water but the enormous flaps used to give extra lift for takeoff were in the up position, and the Flying Boat stayed on the water.

(Below) The flying boat rests quietly on the waters of Long Beach Harbor prior to its first taxi run.

(Inset) Hughes is seen in the cockpit of the giant aircraft wearing his famous brown fedora.

As he approached San Pedro, Hughes eased back on the throttles and the mammoth craft settled back into the water. The Flying Boat had performed perfectly; Hughes smiled broadly; the crew and passengers were excited. Hughes was asked dozens of rapid questions by the accompanying news reporters. Foremost on their minds was whether or not he planned to fly the plane that day. Hughes replied nonchalantly, "No, there are too many systems to be checked out first. I don't intend to do that [fly] for several months. . . ."

The reporters asked to disembark so they could file their stories before deadline. Hughes ordered his P.T. boat to come alongside. Radio newsman Jimmy McNamara watched in distress as the newspaper journalists sped away; he was unable to get his cumbersome recording equipment into the small boat. He cursed his luck, knowing he would be "scooped" by the newspapermen.

As soon as the reporters had disembarked, Hughes ordered one more test run. He turned to Dave Grant and asked for "fifteen degrees flap." Grant was excited; he knew that this was the takeoff setting for the Flying Boat.

The flaps were lowered and Hughes turned the Flying Boat toward the San Pedro end of the harbor. He advanced the throttles. The boat began to accelerate rapidly toward San Pedro.

Jimmy McNamara peered over Hughes' right shoulder and began to call out the Flying Boat's speed from the airspeed indicator on the instrument panel: "We're at thirty-five miles per hour, forty miles per hour. . . over a choppy sea. . . more throttle, fifty-five miles per hour. . . more throttle. . . ." McNamara practically screamed into his microphone to be heard over the roar of the engines and the drumming of the waves upon the hull. Excitement made his voice shrill: ". . . Sixty-five miles per hour. . . we're really moving now. . . seventy miles per hour." McNamara's voice suddenly stopped and for a fraction of a second, silence prevailed—no waves on wood, no roar of engines.

Regaining his voice, McNamara shouted, "And I believe we are airborne! We are airborne, ladies and gentlemen, I don't believe that Howard Hughes meant this to be!"

At seventy miles per hour, the Spruce Goose had lifted gracefully from the waters of Long Beach Harbor and flew—the largest airplane ever to leave the earth's surface. Even the stoic Hughes seemed surprised at the ease with which it lifted into the air.

Dave Grant later recalled that Hughes instinctively jerked back on the throttles when the plane left the water. Hughes knew, of course, that low engine RPM could reduce hydraulic power, so he quickly pushed the throttles forward and then gradually slowed them as the Flying Boat settled smoothly onto the water. The landing was picture perfect, recorded for all posterity by newsreel photographers in attendance.

Jimmy McNamara rushed forward and shouted in Hughes' ear, "Howard, did you intend that?" Hughes turned and reported in his gravelly voice, "Certainly, I like to make surprises."

The Spruce Goose flew a distance of one mile at a maximum altitude of seventy feet. It was airborne for less than one minute, and yet that one brief flight remains one of the most dramatic in aviation history.

A triumphant Hughes taxied the boat back to its berth, right up to its mooring buoy, cutting the engines at the precise moment to allow it to glide to a gentle stop a few feet from its anchor buoy, no small task in the world's largest flying boat. A jubilant Hughes strode up the docking ramp to answer the questions of reporters who crowded around him. The Flying Boat had flown!

Three days after the flight, the Senate hearings in Washington resumed. Even amid new charges and accusations, Hughes was untouchable: the flight of the Spruce Goose had captured the public's hearts. Hughes was once again an aviation hero. The hearings closed anticlimactically on November 22, 1947.

Entombed

After the flight, the Spruce Goose was moored near the Hughes harbor facility while engineers performed post-test checks. Eleven days later, it returned to its dry dock. Hughes originally planned to retest the boat in early 1948, but he wanted design changes that delayed this schedule. His engineers and mechanics worked full-time throughout 1948 and 1949. Several dozen additional engineers were added to help with Hughes' various changes and improvements. (During this period, over 300 people worked on the Flying Boat project.) Hughes even invested $1.75 million in a climate-controlled hangar for the giant seaplane.

Over the ensuing years, Hughes scheduled and

Hughes at the controls of the Spruce Goose during taxi tests on November 2, 1947.

canceled more than a dozen flight dates for the Spruce Goose, and the aircraft was kept on a thirty-day standby alert. But as years passed, it became clear that Hughes' other business interests required most of his attention, although he continued to try to interest the government—unsuccessfully—in the Flying Boat. He continued the project independently, in the meantime spending as much as $1.5 million per year to preserve the boat.

Hughes' staff developed plans for the HFB-2, a metal aircraft—larger than the Flying boat—to be powered by turboprop engines. But it finally became apparent that the concept of giant cargo boats was obsolete and that the Hughes Flying Boat would never fly again. The staff at the harbor site was gradually reduced until there were fewer than a dozen maintenance men who watched over the preservation of the plane. (Even in the last years, the aircraft was kept in perfect condition.)

Hughes considered his Spruce Goose a great personal triumph and he preserved and protected the aircraft as long as he lived. To him, it was a symbol of his youth and of his many accomplishments in the field of aviation.

Howard Robard Hughes, Jr., died on April 5, 1976, in an airplane en route from Acapulco to a hospital in Houston. It seems fitting that a man who gave so much of his life to the achievements of American aviation should spend his last moments in the air.

(Above) The second model of the XF-11 had only one set of propellers on each engine.

(Below, left) Hughes with a model of the Flying Boat in the background, three weeks prior to his successful test.

(Below, right) Hughes pauses beneath the fuselage of the XF-11 prior to boarding the aircraft.

(Opposite, above) Hughes was instrumental in the design of the Lockheed Constellation 049 shown above. This was a radar demonstration for newsmen on May 1, 1947.

The Constellation 049 inspection flight was held in April 1944. Government officials on board included Harry Truman, Owen Brewster, and Homer Ferguson.

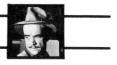

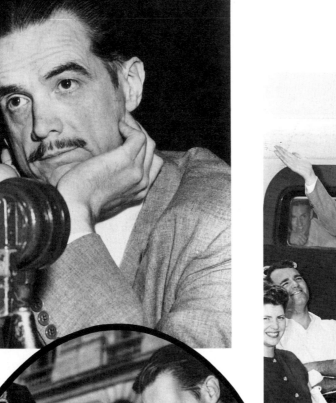

(Above, left) Hughes, partially deaf, used an amplifier to listen to questions during Senate hearings on August 11, 1947, prior to his Spruce Goose flight.

(Above, right) Hughes waves to spectators from the steps of a B-23 at Washington National Airport on his return to California after the 1947 Senate hearings.

(Opposite, above) Hughes and Joseph Bartles at the controls of the Constellation 049, "The Star of California," after landing at La Guardia Airport.

(Opposite, below) Mexican President Miguel Alleman, at the National Palace in Mexico City on February 18, 1947, greets Howard Hughes and Cary Grant, who traveled together to the meeting.

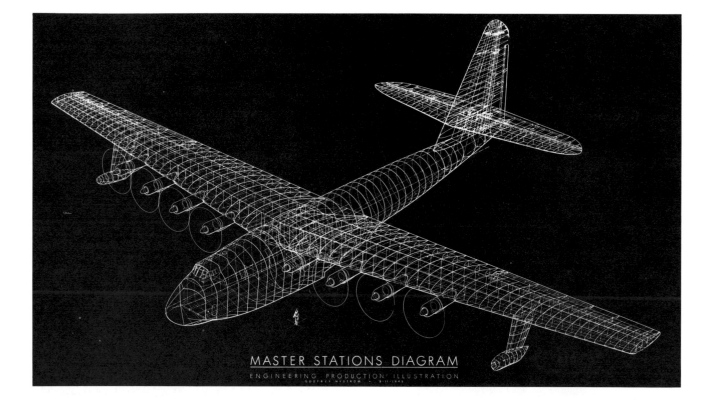

MASTER STATIONS DIAGRAM
ENGINEERING PRODUCTION ILLUSTRATION

(Above) Master Station Diagram shows the complexity of Hughes' Flying Boat structure.

(Below) The Spruce Goose is towed from drydock on November 1, 1947.

(Opposite, above) Hughes, wearing protective shoe covers, inspects generators on Spruce Goose flight deck at Terminal Island, March 1947.

(Opposite, below) Giant Flying Boat rests in 220-foot-long drydock.

(Opposite, above) The cavernous Spruce Goose cargo deck was intended to house 750 troops or two 30-ton Sherman tanks—a total payload of 120,000 journals.

(Opposite, below) Hull moves from hangar at Hughes Aircraft in Culver City, California.

(Inset) Hughes supervises the launch of the Flying Boat from special platform atop the plane's flight deck:

(Below) The Flying Boat is carefully towed from its drydock. Hughes can be seen on platform in background.

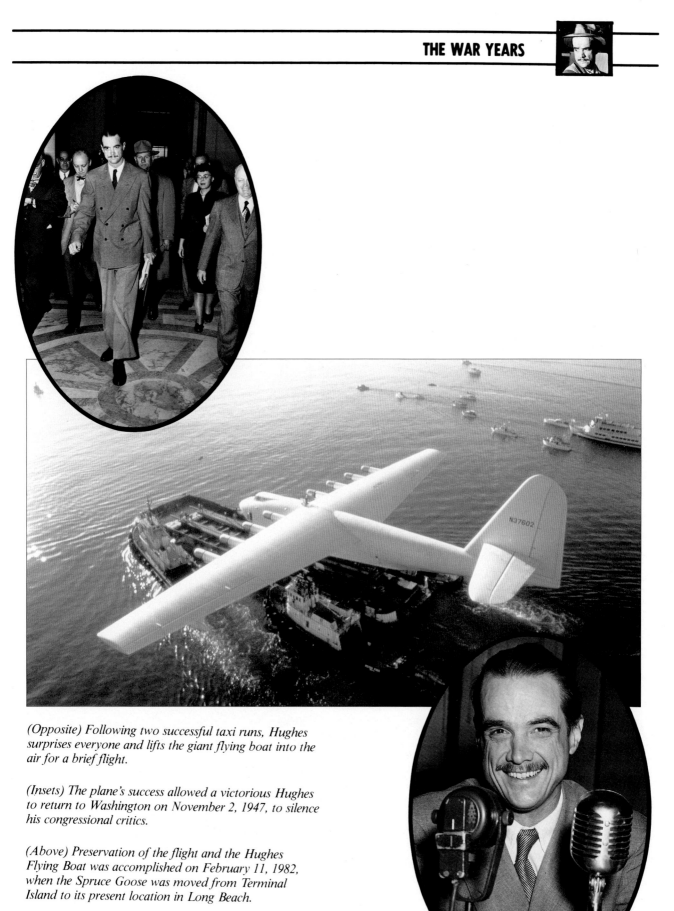

(Opposite) Following two successful taxi runs, Hughes surprises everyone and lifts the giant flying boat into the air for a brief flight.

(Insets) The plane's success allowed a victorious Hughes to return to Washington on November 2, 1947, to silence his congressional critics.

(Above) Preservation of the flight and the Hughes Flying Boat was accomplished on February 11, 1982, when the Spruce Goose was moved from Terminal Island to its present location in Long Beach.

105

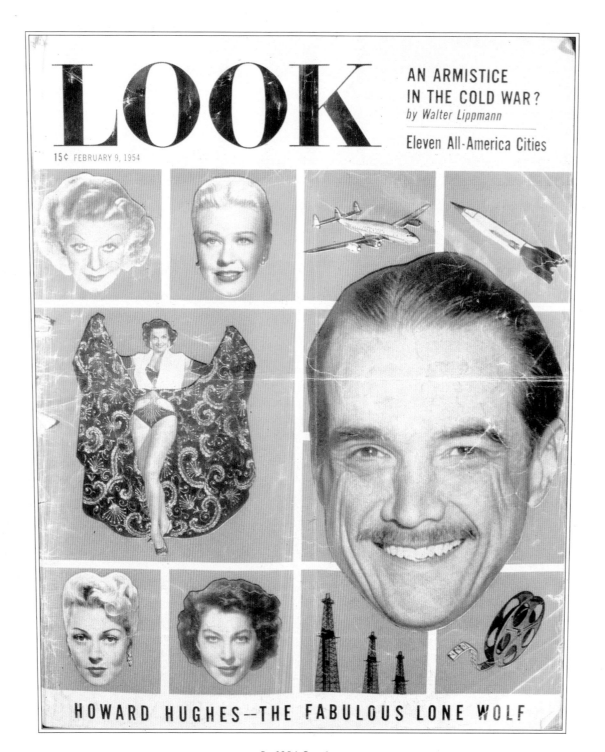

In 1954, Look *magazine ran a feature article on Howard Hughes' life, his achievements and controversies.*

PART FIVE

1947 and Beyond: The Hughes Legacy,

9n 1932, and again in 1935, Hughes had taken time off from his business matters to copilot commercial airliners. In 1932, he flew Fokkermotors for American Airlines' Fort Worth-to-Cleveland run; in 1935 he flew DC-2s for TWA on their transcontinental route. And it was no secret that the purpose of his around-the-world flight in 1938 was to promote the safety, reliability, and value of American transport aircraft. Hughes had prepared meticulously for the trip to demonstrate the ease of long-distance, cross-country, and open-water flights. He set up a worldwide weather-reporting and communications network. He tested new sophisticated electronic guidance and navigation systems.

Hughes began buying TWA stock—at the request of TWA president Jack Frye—in the early 1930s to help finance a reequipment program. By the late 1940s, he owned about 74% of the company's outstanding stock, giving him a controlling interest. One of his first major acts at TWA was to evaluate the company's Boeing 307 Stratoliners (the first four-engine commercial airplanes). One of the planes had recently crashed, revealing serious design defects. TWA and other airlines canceled future orders for more of the 307's, but after lengthy discussions with Boeing engineers, Hughes decided that the problem could be solved. He reinstated TWA's order and the modified Stratoliner proved to be a success.

True to his nature, however, Hughes was not completely satisfied with the Stratoliner: he thought it was too small, too slow, too expensive, and too limited in range. Hughes decided to design a brand new airliner to his own specifications. He wanted a plane that could fly nonstop from Los Angeles to New York with sufficient fuel reserves to fly back to Chicago in case inclement weather prevented landing in New York. He wanted a cruising speed of at least 300 miles per hour, with cabin pressurization for altitudes of 25,000 feet. He wanted an airplane that could carry more than fifty passengers economically

and yet be able to use existing airport facilities. (These were ambitious goals, especially when one realizes that the best airplane in general commercial use at that time was the Douglas DC-3, which cruised at 160 miles per hour and had a range of only 500 miles. In other words, Hughes wanted a speed increase of 87.5% and a range improvement of 600%).

Hughes showed his plans and specifications to different aircraft manufacturers, but each declined the project. Finally, Lockheed agreed to undertake the design and construction—but only if Hughes would foot the bill. Hughes agreed and a team of engineers and designers set out to build this airplane that was years ahead of its time. The final design resulted from the creative minds of many people, including Hughes,

In one of the last known photographs of Howard Hughes, the clean shaven, somewhat heavier billionaire is seen waiting for an elevator in the Los Angeles County Courthouse Hall of Records in 1952.

Jack Frye, and Lockheed's design genius, Clarence (Kelly) Johnson.

The final design called for an advanced passenger transport named the Constellation, or "Connie" for short. It was a four-engine, triple-tailed beauty with a shark-like fuselage. Powered by four 2,500-horsepower Wright Cyclone-18 engines, it could cruise at 25,000 feet (it was capable of flying at 35,000 feet) while maintaining an 8,000-foot air density in the pressurized cabin. The Connie could remain at 25,000 feet on three engines and at 8,000 feet on two engines. The engines were accessible during flight through a passage in the wing, and an engine could be replaced in just thirty minutes by the ground crew. The triple tail was also unique; its vertical height was only twenty three feet, enabling the plane to use existing hangar facilities. (A single tail would have been too large for this convenience.) The airplane incorporated an automatic fire detection system, and special carbon dioxide fire extinguishers were located on the engines. The nacelles and cowlings were made of stainless steel—if an engine fire occurred it could burn for half an hour without seriously hindering the aircraft's operation.

In April 1944, in a highly publicized transcontinental flight (with government inspection officials on board), Hughes crossed the United States in a Constellation from Burbank, California to Washington, D.C. He broke his own H-1 transcontinental record with a time of six hours and fifty-seven minutes.

Unfortunately, Hughes' grand plans for the Constellation were thwarted by the war. As the transports came off the production line, they were requisitioned for military service; thus, TWA was not able to acquire them for its fleet. After the war, however, TWA did use the Constellation on its vast air routes until the jet age made it obsolete.

By 1956, TWA, with its fleet of prop-driven aircraft, began to lose ground to other airlines using the new jet-powered planes. Hughes decided to enter the jet age in his usual grand style: he ordered 33 Boeing 707's, thirty Convair 880's, and an assortment of jet engines. The total bill was $402 million and Hughes suddenly found himself in a tight financial situation. These aircraft purchases and other HFB-1. But the new design was twenty-one feet longer, nearly twice as heavy, and powered by six involvement with TWA ended in a tremendous legal battle in the late 1960s, when, beleaguered by the government and other TWA stockholders, he finally sold his stock. In 1966, he received a check for $546.5 million, the largest single business transaction in financial history.)

Aircraft Division: Hughes Helicopter

To foster his own aviation endeavors, Hughes formed the Aircraft Divsion of the Hughes Tool Company. This entity did not prosper. Hughes' time and energy were widely divided among his many holdings and the Aircraft Division suffered from neglect. The company did receive a few modest military contracts, but these did not even meet the company's overhead costs. The Aircraft Division appeared to be a hobby for Hughes, a place where he could remain active in his beloved field of aviation research.

The engineers at the Aircraft Division worked on a variety of experimental research projects, including designs for various commercial aircraft. One of these designs was for a larger, more modern version of the Hughes Flying Boat. Referred to as the HFB-2, this aircraft would have been made of metal and would have used the same wing and fuselage designs as the HFB-1. But the new design was twenty-two feet longer, nearly twice as heavy, and powered by six turboprop engines. Apparently, the world was not yet ready for jumbo-sized transports; nothing came of the design.

Searching for a worthwhile project, Rea Hopper, the Aircraft Division's top man, set the group working on a design that would forever change the fortunes of the Division. In 1955, Hopper and his team designed a two-seat helicopter, calling it the Model 269 was a light, simple machine, easy to service and maintain. They hoped to sell it to the Army as a light observation helicopter. The Army declined. Undeterred, they began production on the helicopter

(Above) Hughes Aircraft Company at Culver City, California, was the construction site of the Hughes Flying Boat. The large assembly building (to the left of the runway) was the largest wooded structure of its day.

(Right) Hughes stands in front of the XH-17, the world's largest helicopter. It was the first rotary-wing aircraft to test the concept of "hot-cycle" rotor. Hughes is seen with Ray Hopper (right) in Culver City.

(Opposite) A painting portraying the technical diversity of Hughes Helicopters' engineering.

(Right) A military gunship, the Apache, *was built by Hughes Helicopters as a ground support aircraft. The* Apache *won the Collier Award in 1984.*

(Below) Taken at Culver City, this photo shows the enormous size of the XH-17.

in 1956, selling it as a commercial aircraft. Sales volume was low and the project proved to be unprofitable.

Pressing on, the aircraft Division design team went to work on a new concept for yet another light observation helicopter. Their labor was rewarded with an Army contract for the OH-6, six-place helicopter with room in the rear cabin for cargo or for five fully-equipped soldiers. The Model 269A was the forerunner of the Hughes 300, one of the most versatile modern commercial helicopters in use today. An even more sophisticated helicopter also sees worldwide service today—the Hughes 500, which is modeled after the OH-6A.

Hughes also decided to build the world's largest helicopter, a "flying crane," suitable for military use (for air-lifting trucks, jeeps, or artillery) or for commercial use (on construction sites). The XH-17 was not only the largest helicopter in the world, it was also the first to use a hot cycle rotor. (The jet exhaust of the turbine engines was directed through the massive rotor blades, emerging from special jets on the rotor tips and causing the rotation of the blades.) Although the giant flying crane was too expensive to operate economically, it did much to advance the science of rotary-wing aircraft.

Eventually, Hughes Helicopters emerged from the Aircraft Division as its own entity. It has since become one of the world's leading suppliers of both civil and military rotary wing aircraft.

Hughes Helicopters used this model to test the concept of the "hot-cycle" rotor.

Hughes and the Space Age

The aviation companies founded by Hughes have become leaders in aeronautic and astronautic development. Although the billionaire's cherished ambition to produce aircraft for military use was never fully realized, the Aircraft Company has become one of our nation's most important suppliers of complex electronic systems, missiles, satellites, radar tracking devices, and sophisticated weapons control systems.

For example, the first communications satellite to orbit the earth, Earlybird, was a Hughes project; the first U.S. soft landing on the moon was accomplished by Surveyor, a Hughes spacecraft. When the Pioneer mission blasted off for Jupiter, the instruments for two of the scientific experiments aboard were designed by Hughes' Santa Barbara Research Center. The Hughes Helicopter Company is a frontrunner in the field of rotary-wing aircraft and airborne weapons systems. The company supplies the military with light observation helicopters, transports, and advanced gunships; it also markets a competitive line of commercial helicopters worldwide.

This determined, reclusive genius has made many contributions to America and the world; he has left his mark on modern society for all time. Even now, his name is synonymous with power and unparalleled achievement.

A 1950s advertisement shows Hughes' increasing involvement in electronics.

Howard Hughes Medical Institute

Late in 1953, Hughes established the Howard Hughes Medical Institute, a medical research organization begun for "the promotion of human knowledge within the field of the basic sciences and its effective application for the benefit of mankind." He turned over all of the assets and future profits of his Hughes Aircraft Company to the Institute. The Hughes Aircraft Company has since become one of the world's largest and most successful suppliers of complex electronics equipment, missiles, spacecraft and advanced technology and has contributed millions of dollars to medical research.

The first of six Intelsat IV-A telecommunications satellites being prepared for launch by Hughes Aircraft Company of California engineers at the company's Los Angeles facility. This satellite was launched in September 1975.

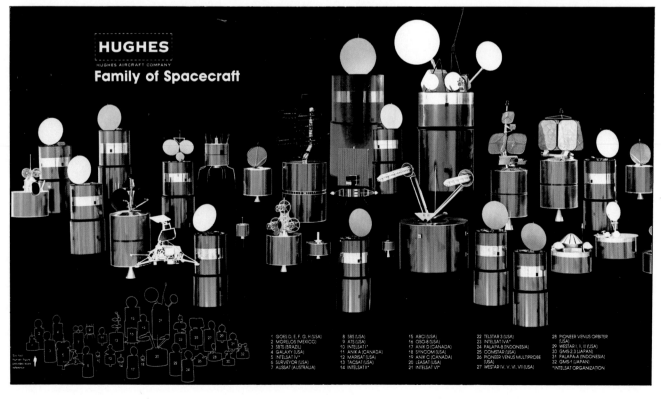

Las Vegas and Hughes Air West

In the later years of his life, Hughes once again entered the airline business, though in a smaller way than his TWA days. He bought a financially ailing commuter service called Air West and renamed it Hughes Air West. Hughes had several reasons for buying this company. First, he had a nostalgic desire to return to the airline business. Second, it made good sense from a business standpoint. In the years before he bought Air West, Hughes had acquired vast holdings in Las Vegas, including several hotels and casinos. Acquisition and successful operation of Hughes Air West would provide good air service into Las Vegas; the airline would also serve as a good public relations tool for the state of Nevada.

Hughes Air West was unique among Hughes' holdings in that it was the only enterprise to use Hughes' name in its advertising. (One ad declared, "There's a new feeling at Air West, and Howard Hughes welcomes you aboard.")

The Spruce Goose Finds a Home

When Howard Hughes died without leaving a signed will, his estate was placed in the courts. In order to preserve the assets for Hughes' heirs, the courts ruled that all unnecessary expenses be curtailed. In Long Beach, the Spruce Goose was still being preserved at a cost of more than $1 million a year. Summa Corporation, Hughes' holding company, was ordered to take steps to dispose of the aircraft. The Smithsonian Institution expressed an interest in the Flying Boat but did not have space to store or display it, nor the means to transport it across the country. Several groups of aviation enthusiasts came forward with plans but no one could come up with sufficient capital to make such an exhibition a reality.

Summa reluctantly planned to disassemble the aircraft and dispose of the pieces. Nine museums, including the Smithsonian, would receive parts of the plane for display. The remainder of the craft would be shredded and destroyed. Across the nation, thousands of aviation enthusiasts were horrified. In 1979, a California-based group, The Committee to Save the Flying Boat, staged demonstrations and rallies and called for support to save the aircraft from destruction. Letters and phone calls deluged local and state politicians, demanding the craft's preservation. The Port of Long Beach briefly examined the possibility of displaying the Hughes Flying Boat, but again, money was a problem: millions of dollars

(Below) The Spruce Goose was maneuvered by tugboat during its first move on October 29, 1980. The planned six-hour move took nearly 36 hours and cost more than $1 million.

would be required to move the aircraft and display it properly.

In the boat's hangar on Terminal Island, the few remaining workmen were preparing to disassemble the craft when at the eleventh hour a saviour appeared. Aroused by the media attention and by his own interest in aviation, Jack Wrather stepped in and offered to save the Spruce Goose. Wrather, an entrepreneur and head of the multi-faceted Wrather Corporation, was owner of the Disneyland Hotel and numerous radio, TV and movie properties, including "The Lone Ranger" and "Lassie." (His wife, Bonita Granville Wrather, was a famous actress in the 1930s and 1940s.) At the time, Wrather had been negotiating with Long Beach for a master lease of the city's financially-troubled tourist attraction, the *Queen Mary*. Wrather felt that the Spruce Goose might be the added attraction that would make the area a

success: the combination of these two greats from the past—the world's largest airplane sitting beside the world's largest ocean liner—might indeed appeal to tourists.

The Spruce Goose would be housed in an appropriate enclosure on the land adjacent to the *Queen Mary*, but an immediate problem surfaced: the Flying Boat would have to be moved at once because its hangar had already been leased to another company. Thus in September 1980, the job of moving the aircraft began. Major settling—nearly twelve feet—had occurred on Terminal Island over the years. This meant that when in water the Spruce Goose would be much higher than when the hangar was originally built. In additon, the rolling doors of the hangar were jammed shut and would not open. Work crews used cutting torches to remove the doors and all parts of the hangar that might touch the

117

airplane when it was floated. The work took nearly two months.

On October 29, 1980, all was ready for the Spruce Goose's "coming out." Fire hoses filled the massive dry dock with sea water in the early morning, and soon she was afloat, bobbing easily in her dock.

A special viewing area had been set up near the hangar where thousands of newsmen and special guests awaited. At 10:30 A.M. the work crews opened the massive steel cofferdam door at the front of the dry dock. As it fell away, the Spruce Goose floated once again on the waters of Long Beach Harbor.

A tugboat, dwarfed by the Flying Boat, attached a line to the seaplane's nose and gently pulled her forward. As the plane's fuselage slowly emerged from the hangar, spectators and workmen waited excitedly. The massive eighty-foot-high tail was nearing the lintel of the hangar door and a collision seemed imminent. But the tail passed through with inches to spare and the Spruce Goose glided majestically into full view. The crowd was ecstatic; throughout the harbor, hundreds of boats sounded whistles and horns. The Goodyear blimp and several news helicopters circled overhead.

The move called for the plane to be towed to a storage site just 600 yards north of the hangar facility, where the aircraft would be lifted on to land by the world's largest self-propelled floating crane, the Navy's YD-171 (affectionately known in Long Beach as Herman the German). A war prize taken from Germany at the end of World War II, it was the only crane on the Pacific Coast that could have lifted the 400,000-pound craft. The special cradle on which the Flying Boat had rested for decades would be removed from the dry dock, attached to lifting beams and placed underwater. The Spruce Goose would be towed into place over the cradle, adjacent to the YD-171, and cables would be lowered into the water and attached to the sunken cradle by divers. The crane would then lift the cradle up underneath the plane's fuselage, where divers would ensure proper alignment before the airplane was lifted into the air and carried across the narrow channel to land.

Problems arose, of course. Two small mobile cranes, trying to lift the heavy cradle out of dry dock, began to sink into the asphalt floor of the hangar. One tipped over, losing its boom in the dry dock. The subsidence so badly undercut the floor of the hangar that the cranes could not get sufficient footing. It took many hours to shore up the floor so that the crane

could finally lift the cradle out of the dry dock. When the cradle was free, it was placed on a special barge where enormous lifting beams were welded to the underside of the cradle. The steel cables from the YD-171 were attached to these lifting beams.

The original schedule called for the move to take six hours, but sunset fell before the cradle was prepared. Workmen labored throughout the night to prepare the lifting equipment. When dawn arrived, the crew was still at work. Throughout that next day, October 30, work continued. Finally, around 8:30 P.M., everything was ready: the Spruce Goose had been towed up the channel and was in place over the submerged cradle. Dozens of men on the giant crane and on shore across the channel held the aircraft in place with strong lines. Divers carefully positioned the cradle under the boat's fuselage. (The beams in the cradle had to match perfectly the struts in the plane's fuselage. If they missed by more than two inches, the plane's fuselage could be crushed.) Underwater cameras enabled the crane commander to ensure perfect positioning of the cradle.

At 8:31 P.M., the commander peered into his video monitor and shouted, "Lift!" Within seconds, the Spruce Goose was airborne for the second time in its career. The crane lifted the enormous boat into the air; it swayed gently as water dripped from its hull. The crane puttered across the narrow harbor channel. The Hughes Flying Boat was lowered to the ground and the lifting cable removed. As the plane touched earth, a tremendous cheer sounded from the workmen and the hundreds of spectators still on hand.

The next morning, crews moved the boat away from the edge of the channel. Here the aircraft was stored for the next sixteen months while work began on its housing structure, located next to the *Queen Mary*.

The Wrather Corporation selected Temcor of Torrance, California, to build the aluminum dome to cover the Spruce Goose. At 415 feet in diameter and 130 feet in height (covering more than three acres), it is the largest clear-span aluminum dome in the world. Construction on the dome began in October, 1981, and by February, 1982, it was ready to house the Spruce Goose.

At 12:01 A.M. on February 11, the German crane once again lifted the Spruce Goose into the air. This time the boat was lowered onto a specially prepared barge. At dawn, tugboats nudged the Spruce Goose along its final journey, five nautical miles from

(Left) Seen from the inside of the giant aluminum dome, the Spruce Goose waits to be brought on land.

(Below) The Spruce Goose as seen today inside its permanent installation.

Terminal Island to Pier J. Hundreds of small boats trailed while spectators lined the shore to watch the last move of this great craft. She arrived offshore near the stern of the *Queen Mary,* where her barge was aligned with a steel drawbridge. Anchors and guy lines steadied the barge as the Spruce Goose was towed tail-first onto land. As the boat's massive eight-story tail slid under the edge of the dome, crowds cheered and boats sounded their whistles. At exactly 12:31 P.M., the Spruce Goose was safely on land.

Work on the Hughes Flying Boat Exhibition continued through 1982, and on May 14, 1983, the Spruce Goose opened to the public.

During the three decades that the Spruce Goose was hidden away on Terminal Island, fewer than 300 outsiders saw her. When the Spruce Goose opened to the public, thousands waited in line; and has since been seen by millions, a fitting tribute to the aircraft's special place in aviation history.

Shortly after the Spruce Goose's famous 1947 flight, Hughes had sent a photograph of the plane in flight to Eloi J. Amar of the Long Beach Harbor Department. In the inscription, Hughes thanked Amar for his help in preparing for the flight and wrote: "I hope someday Long Beach will regard this plane with a certain amount of pride." This sentiment may very well be the only true last will and testament of Howard Robard Hughes. It is a desire expressed from the heart, a desire that is coming true in Long Beach today as millions marvel at this special aircraft built by an extraordinary man.

The Spruce Goose is gently nudged by tugboats toward its new home in the world's largest clear-span aluminum dome. The Queen Mary is docked beside it. (Inset) Inside the Spruce Goose exhibit, visitors view a cutaway model of the Pratt 7 Whitney R-43 engine.